Sean Bridle;

Sean Bricelle,

WILTSHIRE

Edited by Claire Tupholme

First published in Great Britain in 2003 by
YOUNG WRITERS
Remus House,
Coltsfoot Drive,
Peterborough, PE2 9JX
Telephone (01733) 890066

All Rights Reserved

Copyright Contributors 2003

HB ISBN 1 84460 168 4
SB ISBN 1 84460 169 2

FOREWORD

Young Writers was established in 1991 as a foundation for promoting the reading and writing of poetry amongst children and young adults. Today it continues this quest and proceeds to nurture and guide the writing talents of today's youth.

From this year's competition Young Writers is proud to present a showcase of the best poetic talent from across the UK. Each hand-picked poem has been carefully chosen from over 66,000 'Hullabaloo!' entries to be published in this, our eleventh primary school series.

This year in particular we have been wholeheartedly impressed with the quality of entries received. The thought, effort, imagination and hard work put into each poem impressed us all and once again the task of editing was a difficult but enjoyable experience.

We hope you are as pleased as we are with the final selection and that you and your family will continue to be entertained with *Hullabaloo! Wiltshire* for many years to come.

CONTENTS

Felix Fiducia-Brookes	38
Joshua Charlesworth	38
Toby Wood	39
Alexander Lawrence	39

Crockerton Primary School

Christy Blance	40
Emilea Whatley-Gibbs	40
Claudia Hickin	41
Harry Baldwin	41
Rhiannon Daly	42
Bee Lee	42
Emily Jones	43
Lucy Gunter	44
James Scott Palmer	44
Felicity Webb	45
Aaron Teager	45
George Baldwin	46
Curtis Saunders	46
Alyssa Piper	47
Kristie Cockayne	47
Felicity House	48
Christina Webb	48
Joe Ramsden	49
Sophie Minter	50
Sam Whatley-Gibbs	50
Jay Potter	51
Hannah Manson	51
Georgina Henry	51
Siân Madge	52
Jordan Henry	52
Alexandra Muir	53
Robyn Harding	53
Tom Lewis	54
Nick Legg	54
Ben Clough	54

Derry Hill CE Primary School

Siân Rowley	55
Alice Nolan	56
Hannah Massey	57
Lauren Seager	58
Daisy Payne	59

Forest & Sandridge Primary School

Naomi Jackson	60
Hazel Travers	60
Natalie Bourne	61
Zoe Meakin	61
Jessica Dobson	61
Richard Everett	62
Dan Moore	62
Rebecca Blackey	63

Freshbrook Primary School

Daniel Hughes	63
Andrew Nutt	64
Lucas Gillett	64
Ka-Yan Cheung	64
Faye Millin	65
Rebecca Smyth	65
Priyanka Joshi	65
Alexandra Lee	66
Katie Stevens	66
Carmen-Thea Harper	66
Megan Poppy	67
Hannah Gale	67
Josh McHugh	68
Joe Shepherd	68
Chloe Roberts	69
Gemma Louise Scott	69

Heytesbury Primary School

Jamie McDougall	70
Nathan Bond	70

Jessica Agate	70
Liam Beattie	71
Scott Lewis	71
Rebecca Newman	72
Ben Agate	72
Daniel Bone	73
Sasha Bowen	73
Heather Newman	74
Thomas Dalby	74
Alex Merx	75
Emily Whitcombe	75
Samantha Grindley	76
Emma Reade	76
Molly Stuart	77
Lauren Pinnell	77
Caitlin Skeates	78

Kingsbury Hill House School

Florence Corp	78
Matthew Dyas	79
Victoria Bushell	80
Poonam Mandalia	80
Philippe Clayton	81
Kishan Patel	81
Tristan Cotterill	82
Magella Oldcorn	82
Ella Cochran-Patrick	83
Christopher Dyas	83
Philip Williams	84
Patricia Grove	84
Sonali Patel	85
Nicholas Dawes	85
Ciara Connell	86
Kit Williams	86
Thomas Dawes	87
Richard Martin-Barton	88
Rebecca Drew	88

Hannah Hollis	88
Abigail Bullock	89
Freddie Corp	89
Alex Hill	90
Samantha Ockwell	90
Sophie Mattick	91

Langley Fitzurse CE Primary School

Kirsty Tyler	91
Maddy Dann	92
Alexis Wormald	92
Jessica Fairbairn	93
Dewi Evans	94
Sophie Chalmers	95
Victoria Seales	96
Miriam Stiglitz	96
Mike Flynn	97
Chenise Austin	98
Amy Stutt	98
Chantelle Chapman	99

La Retraite Swan

Peter Drake	99
James Cole	99
Thomas Newman	100

Luckington Community School

Jacob Simpkins	100
Rebecca Thompson	101
Kathryn Hutchinson	101
Jake Beckett	102
Elizabeth Hutchinson	102
Caroline Kyle	102
Harrison Moore	103
Jamie Jobbins	103
Jennifer Baron	104
Abigail Boulton	104

St Andrew's CE Primary School, Swindon

Eleanor Ridge	122
Holly Goldsmith	122
Emily Harrison	123
Sophie Lloyd	123
Jack Thompson	124
Georgie Castle	124
Chris Walker	125
Angellina Marie Nagitta	125
Hannah Carter	126
Matthew Sweeney	126
Stephanie Moore	126
Adam Beasant	127
Hannah Glass	127
James Fairclough & Josh Jones	128
Sophie Bell	128
Samantha Cowie	129

St George's School, Warminster

Bryony Mason	129
Rory Walsh	130
Cristina Fordham	130
Philippa Wall	131
Adam Holman	131
Alexandra Andow	132
Dominque Aston	133
Sarah Devoy	134
Charles Allardice	134
Cariad Wright	135
James Baysting	135
Kyle Byrne	136
Hannah Rea	136
Abi Blagdon	137
Ellen Tansey	137
Yasmin Galbraith	138
Emma Hutchinson	138
Ashley Holman	139

St John's RC School, Trowbridge

Joseph Burrows	140
Jack Rosier	140
Peter Hammond	141
Sarah Devereux	141
Stephanie McGee	142
Nick Rodgerson	143
Gemma Giles	143
Sean Patrick Bridle	144
Lauren Binder	144
Emma Bracey	145
Faye Vanstone	145
Charlotte Waller	146
Hannah Anderson	146
Thomas Miller	147
Simon Stafford	147
Sarah Jones	148
Christopher Raymond	148

Sarum St Paul's Primary School, Salisbury

Stacey Vincent	148
Catherine Simpson	149
Jacob Stanistreet	149
James Neville	150
Rebecca Baker	150
Jennifer Dawson	151
Poppy Short	151
Lorraine Dawson	152
Jack Stead	152
Stephanie Hatchman	153
Melissa Crouch	153
Michael Shaw	154
Alicia Murphy	154
Lauren Crockett	154
Louis Bennett	155
Conor Sheehan	155
Scott Biddle	155
Lauren Anthony	156

Sherston CE Primary School

The Poems

WHAT AM I?

An undiscovered den
Waiting, watching.
Snap,
Crackle,
Pop.
Running, screaming,
A red ribbon.
Thrashing, spiralling,
Suffocating me.
The landscape swallows,
It explodes
Like a cascading waterfall.
Screams echo,
Waiting, waiting
To be part of a world.
We all bow down in its wake,
Snap,
Crackle,
Pop.
Drawing me in,
Tumbling, wafting, swaying.
It has taken over
Our world.
Dying,
Dying.
A volcano.

Gemma Roots (11)
Amesbury Junior School

WHAT COULD I BE?

A deep-sea diver I would be,
Beneath the waves, the things I'd see,
I'd walk along the seabed,
Where I would see the things he said.

Perhaps NASA I will be,
To see the things that astronauts see,
I'd sail through space,
Without a trace.

Maybe a swimmer is really me,
To swim across the open sea,
Dodging fish,
To make a wish.

A writer I could be,
To write about the sea
And all the weirdness that happened there,
Could it be a dragon's lair?

Ben Lister (10)
Amesbury Junior School

THE SEA

Sparkling in the sunset like diamonds on a ring,
Ripples in the rain,
Reflection in the sun,
Dolphins jumping in the water,
Calling to each other,
People on the stony, yellow beach,
Watching people bodyboarding and surfing,
Children playing, people swimming,
Everyone having fun!

Louise Sleeman (9)
Amesbury Junior School

THE FOUR SEASONS

Fresh new flowers,
April showers,
Lots of light,
When the sun shines bright.

Sun shining every day,
Lots of fun swimming in the bay,
Thrilling holidays,
Better than being in a maze.

Leaves falling off trees,
In the light breeze,
Small creatures nesting near their food,
Don't be in that dreadful mood.

Cold and white, thick snow,
Why can't it go to your toe?
Scarf, gloves, the whole kit,
I've got a big mitt!

Catherine Steer (10)
Amesbury Junior School

ON THE PRAIRIE

Stripes flash behind swaying grass,
Lions laze under shady trees, while lionesses hunt,
Scouring the bleak landscape,
To feed hungry offspring,
Cheetahs sprint after antelope
That leap and kick up red dust,
Dust that blurs images,
The heat is intense,
I struggle on.

Tamsin Pamby (9)
Amesbury Junior School

TWO MINUTES TO 9 O'CLOCK

Two minutes to 9 o'clock
I'm still not asleep
And these things I think:
Why are my feet so cold?
Shall I put my headphones on and listen to a CD?
Oh no, I'm going to miss my favourite TV programme
I'll never get to sleep because I'm so bored
Shut up Matty, you're snoring

One minute to 9 o'clock
And these things I think:
What is the weather like outside?
I can smell my mum and dad's tea
I wonder what we will do at school tomorrow?
Shall I go and get a book?
(I better not in case I stand on a creaky floorboard)
It is 21:00 and still
No changeeeeee . . . .

Timothy Anderson-Emm (9)
Amesbury Junior School

IF I WAS A . . .

If I was a talented dolphin
I'd swim and ponder or write a hymn
Perhaps I'd compose a symphony
Or write my autobiography

If I was an educated frog
Sat upon a sunken log
I'd learn to read and write my name
And win every Monopoly game

If I was a comic giraffe
Making lots of people laugh
I'd be dame of the pantomime
Or perhaps involved in a serious crime.

Jemma Barwick (11)
Amesbury Junior School

SAMMY THE SUPER SNAIL

You may not think this is quite right,
But every day and every night . . .
Sammy the super snail loves to run,
She'll win a race at the bang of a gun.

She'd win this and she'd win that,
Once, she even raced a cat!

It was a sunny day then, ten years ago,
A small breeze,
Trees swaying
To and fro.

She ran so fast around the track,
That everything was a blur,
She left all her cares back at the starting line,
So she didn't mind what occurred.

She won the race just as she wished,
Then along came a human
And she got *squished!*

Georgina Dingwall (11)
Amesbury Junior School

The Dolphin

The water like shattered glass was
Still
Still
Still
As the sun sank down
Down
Down in the distance
Then suddenly
An elasticated body of a trapeze artist
Sprang into action
Leaping, springing on the distant horizon
Twisting, twirling, all rolled into one . . .
Then he vanished.
Gone
Gone
Gone!

Trudi Bull (10) & Hattie Taylor (11)
Amesbury Junior School

My Puppy

When my puppy jumps up
She makes me drop my cup
Sometimes, she is so strong
That she can pull me along

She is so cuddly
When she's not muddy
Smooth, silky fur
She's the best, that's for sure.

Philipa Fautley (10)
Amesbury Junior School

FOG

It's coming, it's coming,
Down,
Down,
Down.
Swoosh!
Like a smokescreen,
Hiding secrets,
Swooping,
Sliding,
Tumbling,
A ghostly galleon
On the waves,
Down,
Down,
Down.

Shaun Darragh (10)
Amesbury Junior School

THE GALLOPING HORSE

A misty night, a horse breaks out
A strawberry sunrise
Galloping, dancing hooves
Into the unknown
My breath like steam makes trails in the cold air
Dizzy, dancing, diamond
Gaunt trees beckon
Images pass in a blur
The sunlight blinds me
I gallop towards the horizon.

Louise Richards (9)
Amesbury Junior School

ROLLER COASTER

Up and down
Round and round
See the sky
And then the ground

Feeling frightened
Feeling scared
Can't believe it
I really dared

Hair-raising
Stomach-churning
Forget the candyfloss
I was yearning

Legs wobbling
Hand shaking
What a fuss
We've all been making!

Ann-Marie Hazzard (10)
Amesbury Junior School

THE DRAGONFLY

Her wings are cut glass
Darting above the dark lake
She swoops and hovers
Shimmers of green, crystal-blue
Like a tiny glass window.

Amy Greaves (10)
Amesbury Junior School

ALIENS

Aliens, aliens, aliens
Walking through space
Aliens, aliens, aliens
With spots all on their face

Aliens, aliens, aliens
What an ugly sight
Aliens, aliens, aliens
Glowing in the light

Aliens, aliens, aliens
In their little ship
Aliens, aliens, aliens
Going on a trip

Aliens, aliens, aliens
Coming to say hello and hi
Aliens, aliens, aliens
Hope they'll soon say *goodbye!*

Annette Matthews (11)
Amesbury Junior School

DOGS

If I was a dog
I would stay out in the fog
I would stay out all night
And maybe fly a kite.

Amy Glasson (10)
Amesbury Junior School

DOLPHINS

The gymnast spinning
Turning, gliding effortlessly
Into the waves
Of the deep, dark sea
Full of secrets

This magical ballerina
Shoots out of the sun-drenched ocean
Dances through the air
Nose-dives back into
The deep, dark sea
Full of secrets.

Ruth Dalley (10)
Amesbury Junior School

GROWING UP!

I used to be a bonny baby
And bounce and coo all day

I used to be a terrible toddler
And throw my toys away

I used to be a sweet young thing
But then a tantrum I would fling

I used to be an awful child
But I'm all grown up now and

Wild, wild, wild!

Amy Collier (10)
Amesbury Junior School

LOST IN THOUGHTS
(Inspired by the book 'I am David')

I'm lost in thoughts
I really am
Thoughts are harmful
Am I insane?

I dream of getting out of this place
I've bruises on my ribs and back
I wake up to find a German flag
Am I mad?

Grey and damp and dark
Like my thoughts
My surroundings harbour
My innermost soul
Don't let me go mad.

Lewis Lennane-Emm (10)
Amesbury Junior School

PETS

Horses, hamsters, guinea pig, dog
Cat, rabbit, toad and frog
All of these animals can be pets
But of course you may have regrets
Jumping and playing in the summer's sun
Running and skipping and having fun
Squealing, sniffing, things that tear and rip
Running, jumping and doing a front flip
This is the end of my pet rhyme
Don't worry, they shouldn't commit a terrible crime.

Toni Austin (11)
Amesbury Junior School

DREAMS

I'd be a worldwide famous singer
I'd star in Austin Powers, the movie swinger
I'd hang out with S Club and Avril Lavigne
I'd only be in my teens

My dad would get some of my money
He'd buy instruments all made of brass
Whilst my brother would be an international wrestling star,
kicking butt
Now my mum, what would she get? A diamond cookery set
I think to myself, *should this happen?*
I'd give every kid a pet.

Joseph Mark Dunford (9)
Amesbury Junior School

WALKING HOME

The sun shines on the beautiful red swing,
Just as the school bell's about to ring,
I run home all alone across the bright green grass,
I run straight under the sun,
I'm there,
The only thing I can do is stand and stare,
Is it me
Or can I
See the sea?
Is it me or can I see the sea?

Rachel Muirhead & Michaela Hill (9)
Amesbury Junior School

THE SEED EATER

There was once a very silly boy who swallowed pips and seeds
He never spat them out again and soon they grew like weeds

Inside him there were melon plants, plums and bananas too
But why these things were growing there, no one ever knew . . .

Until one day when from his ear a leafy thing appeared
And his best friend said, 'Goodness me, that looks a little weird!'

What can it be? It's small and green and curly at the end
The boy was baffled, what on earth had happened to his friend?

The doctor said, 'I do declare, I think this is a tree,
But I can't imagine how such a thing could be.'

The boy then said, 'I think you're right and there is something more -
My other ear feels rather strange and actually quite sore.'

The doctor looked and felt around and said with some dismay
'Yes, something strange is growing there, I don't know what to say!'

By the weekend, the little boy had fruit and nuts galore
From both his ears and nose as well, all falling on the floor

His friends came round and feasted and said, 'You lucky chap,'
But he replied, 'It's not such fun, I haven't had a nap

For seven days, I can't lie down you see, or I will break
The branches and there won't be any fruit and nuts to take.'

Eventually of course they had to prune those trees
And pull them out from his poor nose, they made him want to sneeze

The moral of this lengthy rhyme is *pips and seeds must stay
Upon your plate*, cos otherwise you could go the same way!

Emily Sims (10)
Avondale School

A Cautionary Tale

Moral: Never play with matches

Little Lucy plays with matches
And on fire she always catches,
One day her mother told her,
'Always listen to someone older!'

Lucy didn't listen to this
And lit a match which made a hiss,
Almost at once she caught on fire,
Her situation was quite dire!

Little Lucy ran to the doctor
And in a freezing cold bath he had locked her,
In five minutes she was cured,
But then into a cave she was lured . . .

She lit a match to light her way
And found a friend who said, 'Let's play!'
In two seconds flat, she was alight,
Crying and shouting into the night!

Lucinda Green (10)
Avondale School

FIREBOLT

Clickety-clack along the tracks
Oh, how the steam train goes,
She puffs, she hisses and makes a jolt
Brakes off and whistle blows.

Along the tracks, under the bridge
It's a really amazing sight,
The sun reflects off her coat
The effect is extremely bright.

Look out the window, see some hills
On one is Little Bo Peep!
But something's missing, do you know?
I know! It's her sheep!

A burst of steam, a screech of steel
The train, she's slowing down
And finally she comes to a halt
Wheels now stopped going round.

Harriet McClure (9)
Avondale School

NEVER PLAY NEAR WATER

Moral: Never play near water

Lily Jonson was her name
Catching fish was her favourite game
All of her friends said she was *lame*
But she thought it was worth the fame

One day she came across a pond
Of which she knew she was quite fond
Then suddenly it all went wrong
She fell in, with a screaming song

Her granny went off like a mortar
And said, 'You mischievous granddaughter
And seeing you so wet and cold
It makes me feel so very old'

She was so shaken by the fall
She never went back there at all
Thankfully they've built a fence
It cost them lots in pounds and pence.

Marcus Broom (11)
Avondale School

A CAUTIONARY TALE

Moral: Never play with knives

The suffering of Edward Ives,
Was playing with his father's knives.
Whilst standing in the butcher's shop,
He spied a very juicy chop.

His daddy owned that little store,
But he went through the shop's back door.
Leaving Eddie all alone,
Just him and an old chicken bone.

Now this is when young Ed picks up
The biggest knife he'd seen
And being of the violent sort,
Thought he was in a dream.

'I think I'll cut this steak in two,'
The little boy did call,
But he looked out the huge window
And cut his hand off, whole.

The moral of this woeful tale,
About poor Edward Ives,
When you're not looking at the blade,
Don't play with Daddy's knives.

Jenny Ridley (11)
Avondale School

WHAT HAVE I DONE TO DESERVE THIS?

There was a dolphin all alone,
Looking at its destroyed home,
One day the dolphin was struggling to swim at sea,
Thinking what has man done to me?

There was a fish all alone,
Looking at its destroyed home,
People here destroy river banks,
All the rivers are polluted by oil tanks.

Danielle Parkes (9)
Avondale School

FRANKENSTEIN

Frankenstein was on his bed
with an arrow right through his head
and a sharp knife through his chin
but still he wore a nasty grin

He had a patch upon his eye
and after that he could not lie
he had two bolts right through his neck
and you should see his house, a wreck

His skin was green with boils red
he even had some on his head
he had a bruise and scars quite bad
and had four teeth which seems quite mad

His hair was scruffy, black and grey
his ear stuck out like wheat or hay
his claws were long with blood all over
and his car was just a little Rover

He ate all the children who passed by
well, only ten-year-olds tell a lie
he cooked them in soup with sugar and spice
and sometimes ate them with chicken and rice.

Dale Mundell (10)
Avondale School

LIZZY'S TEETH

Lizzy loved to eat and eat
anything that tasted sweet
but the one thing that she'd forgotten
is that her teeth would soon be rotten

She went to the dentist to have a filling
the dentist said, 'Tut, tut' and started drilling
he drilled and drilled and drilled
until the hole was completely filled

She went back home to eat some cake
but her mum said, 'An hour you must wait'
so she looked in the cupboard and started to forage
and while she was digging she came across porridge

There is a moral to this story
it really makes you quite snorey
the moral is that you should never, ever
have too many sweets, whatever the weather.

Coraleigh Saunders (10)
Avondale School

THE HOGWARTS EXPRESS

As I totter down the platform, golly gosh, it's Harry Potter
I also see Rebeus Hagrid looking like a ragged owl
As I was getting on the train, I saw a boy with hair like a flame
Then finally it's time to go, the whistle is about to blow
As we were on our way to the school
With our wands we were being fools

Doing magic and having fun, the journey had just about begun
The train was going really fast, we could see the steam blowing past
Out of the window I could see lambs and sheep, standing under a tree
The train was making a chuffing sound
The wheels were going round and round
We finally got there, the journey ends
And I got off the train with my friends.

Sarah Lunt (10)
Avondale School

THE INDIAN EXPRESS

The train is working very hard
On the platform stands the guard
He holds a whistle in his palm
He has a flag under his arm

Now the train is about to start
It sounds like the beating of a heart
Lots of steam pours out of the funnel
Watch as it goes through a tunnel!

England Ireland, Scotland, Wales
All have trains that run on rails
You can go wherever you like
You can even take your bike!

I love to travel on a train
Even if it's in the rain
The countryside whizzes by
All in the twinkle of an eye!

Hattie Le Gresley (9)
Avondale School

MY GREAT WHITE SHARK

Blue as the sky,
Teeth as sharp as kitchen knives,
Swimming through the vast blue sea,
Hunting for a human being -
Then he will rip it to pieces or slices,
When he's finished his mega prize,
He goes to find his best pals,
Hammerhead and the cookiecutter
And the whale shark,
The basking shark and the lemon shark,
The angel shark and last but not least,
The grey reef shark,
What am I?
I'm the great white shark,
King of the sea.

Charlie Ward (10)
Avondale School

FISH HUNT

Dolphins swimming freely
Trying to catch some fish
Herd them up quickly
Then one by one
Eat the fish but
Don't eat them all at
Once otherwise
They would have
To start the hunt again.

Thomas Dhanji (10)
Avondale School

A CAUTIONARY TALE

Moral: Do not steal

There was a young girl called Camilla
Who wanted a tiny chinchilla
She got to the shop but she had no more money
So she stole the rodent in panic and hurry

Once home, it was put in its cage
When her parents burst in with rage
She hadn't received their most gracious permission
And so she was sent to spring-clean the kitchen

The next day went not at all well
The police came and rang the doorbell
They ordered Camilla to give back the rodent
She didn't, so they had to call the President
She was arrested, 'Don't wait'
Said the President, 'Don't hesitate'

She is now in jail wearing black and white
And cries on her bed every night
Her parents don't visit
The house looks exquisite
So let that be a lesson, so please don't
Go and steal a tiny rodent
Or you will end up like Camilla
Who wanted a tiny chinchilla.

Verity Cameron (11)
Avondale School

MY FAMILY

Saturday's arrived
Now school is out
Here is my family
Mucking about

Into the garage
Here is my dad
Fixing a shelf
For his big lad

Now in the kitchen
Mum is making cakes
First in the oven
And now it bakes

Climbing up the stairs
The first brushstroke
Hannah is an artist
It isn't a joke

Down the corridor
I hear music play
David is practising
Nearly every day

As I look out my window
I hear the birds sing
One sits on a branch
As it spreads its wing

In Rebekah's room
It is in a mess
Clothes on the floor
Surprisingly, a dress.

Naomi Clarke (9)
Avondale School

LOST FOREVER

A long time ago when we used to play, my whale friend and me,
The male whales have been taken away
But now it's only me, I think he has forgotten me
Struggling through the gloom, this doom is getting closer
Can't man leave me alone? I'm just getting so forlorn
Can't anyone help me, man keeps putting poison in my
Once beautiful home.

Karina Roche (10)
Avondale School

THE FISH

Once I had a small pet fish,
Who swam in my mum's dish.
One day I saw him on the floor
And he was heading for the door!
I ran upstairs to tell my mum,
She said, 'Oh God! Where's my gun?'
Through the door and down the lane,
We could see this fish would be a pain!
He was heading for our neighbour's house,
The neighbour thought he was a mouse.
Through the woods and down the lane,
Then we went into the woods again!
When the fish got tired out,
My mum started to shout,
'Now!' she said, 'You must die,
I'll put you in a fishy pie.'
'Oh no,' said the fish, 'this is bad,
It will make my parents very sad.'

William Edwards & Daniel Mackintosh (11)
Burbage Primary School

THE CLEANER

There once was a cleaner
Who lived in a mop
He was filthy and grubby
And covered in slop

With flies flying round him
All day and night
He smelt like the sewers
And was a terrible sight

There once was a cleaner
Who never worked hard
He didn't get paid
And he only ate lard!

This terrible cleaner
Is nasty and old
He always wears clothes
And still gets cold!

Ben Lay (10) & Jonathan Street (11)
Burbage Primary School

MY CUDDLY TOY

He's friendly and cuddly
And so very soft,
He stays by my side
And I never hear him cough,
He glides across my bed,
To play with the other toys,
When we go to sleep,
He never makes a noise.

Christie Strong (9)
Burbage Primary School

RUBBISH DUMP

Down in the rubbish dump,
Where mice hide,
There's an old, rusty kettle
And a dirty, old slide.

Down in the rubbish dump,
Where rats live,
There's an old, smelly pan
And a rotten kitchen sieve.

Down in the rubbish dump,
Where crisp packets scatter,
There's an old tin can
And a load of litter.

Down in the rubbish dump,
Where frogs jump,
There's a smelly broken ball
And an old tyre pump.

Down in the rubbish dump,
Where diggers crash and boom,
There's a dustpan and brush
And a broken broom.

Down in the rubbish dump,
Where flies buzz,
There's an old man's coat
And a seat from a bus.

Louise Feakes (8)
Burbage Primary School

JANUARY

Frost on the bricks that cracks like a piece of glass
The snow that has fallen on the ice-cold grass

The moon that speaks, goes round and round
Like leaves on a tree that whisper no sound

The snow falls like berries from a tree
While ice slips slowly as can be

The breath of the mist flies like a bird
As the metal on the gate makes no word!

Laura Davenport (10)
Burbage Primary School

JANUARY BRINGS THE SNOW

January brings the snow
Makes you walk very slow

The grass shines like the bright sun
Makes me want a hot cross bun!

Walk out the door to a white wonderland
It makes you feel very grand

The trees sway in the breeze
No more the hum of the bees.

Lucy Foster (10)
Burbage Primary School

THE SNAKE

The snake is a long creature
The snake is a desert creeper
The snake is a scaly thing
The snake is not thin

The snake is an egg eater
The snake is a mouse beater
The snake is a tree climber
The snake is a meat diner.

Rachel Stockwell (8)
Burbage Primary School

SEA POEM

The skilful fish who avoid the stone
Are chased by a shark who's on his own,
Underwater is a dangerous place,
Down there you won't see a friendly face,
Seaweed sways as the breeze
Sweeps through the underwater land with ease,
But not a sound disturbs the ocean floor,
For there is not a door
To the underwater place,
There's no escape from the chase.

James Barlow (10)
Burbage Primary School

CHRISTMAS TIME

C hristmas is a time for fun
H elping and caring for everyone
R unning around in the snow
I heard the tradition *Ho! Ho! Ho!*
S anta Claus went through the sky
T o my surprise he threw me a pie
M e and my mum said, 'Thank you very much.'
A nd what a surprise, he threw my rabbit's present, obviously a hutch
S o my Christmas was the best ever and was for my rabbit as well.

Victoria Adams (10)
Burbage Primary School

THE SEA

I see a whale passing by;
Its skin glistening by the sea.

I see a school of fish;
Their bright colours standing out.

I see tons of bright coral;
The colours of a rainbow.

I see waves crashing on the ground;
There is lots of foam.

I see a boat sailing by;
There are some fenders on the side.

Jessica Mundy (10)
Burbage Primary School

WINNIE THE POOH

Winnie the Pooh is just the best,
He's better than all the rest.
He's sweet as honey,
Cuddlier than a bunny
And yellow and sunny.

Winnie the Pooh is my best friend,
Mine and his friendship will never end.
He's always at the end of my bed,
But when I go to sleep,
He's cuddled up near my head.

Rachel Mackintosh (9)
Burbage Primary School

GREEN

Green makes me think of spring,
New leaves on trees,
Fresh peas,
Holly trees.
Green makes me think of long, wet grass,
Swaying in the wind.
Mint ice cream,
Broccoli green,
Green makes me think of a Christmas tree,
With silver and gold balls on it.
Lettuce leaves,
Sour limes,
Frogs jumping from tree to tree,
Avocados,
Apples,
Grass snakes slithering,
That's what green makes me think of.

Ana Rose Critchley (10)
Calder House School

FIREWORK NIGHT

Catherine wheels hiss and sizzle,
Green and red rockets swoosh up in the sky,
Bang, boom, swoosh they go,
Screamers shoot up and scream in the air,
Sparklers hiss, sizzle and fizz.
The bonfire roars and crackles,
I stand and watch the firelight,
Until it is time to go,
It's the best night ever.

Toby Underwood (8)
Calder House School

BEDTIME

I got into bed
I heard something creaking
I looked . . .
And there wasn't anything there!
There was a shadow,
I couldn't get to sleep,
Owls were hooting,
I heard the gate creaking,
I heard dogs barking,
I hid under my covers,
Bedtime was so long!
Something was crawling up my bed . . .
It licked me!
It was my cat,
I was safe now.

Christopher Wright (11)
Calder House School

FROST

He walks in a hailstorm,
Winter is his season,
He is strong and big,
Early in the morning, he creeps stealthily
And turns our island into ice,
But when the sun comes, he runs!
His only friends are Snow and Ice,
When they are together,
They turn our world
Into a frosty paradise.

Charles Collins (11)
Calder House School

KITTEN

The kitten is outside,
His name is Carrot.
His fur is ginger,
But his eyes are blue.
His tail sways in the wind,
He hisses,
His fur spikes up,
He swipes his paw,
Arches his back
And leaps upon his enemy.
Hiss! Spit!
Miaow!
The fight is over.
Carrot is back on the window sill
As if nothing had happened.
That's cats!

Stephen Hynes (11)
Calder House School

THE LEMMING

I see a lemming
Just bigger than a guinea pig
Ferreting for food in the long grass
Suddenly an owl takes flight
The lemming sees it
And he bolts over the cliff
At the bottom
It is raining with lemmings
Gliding to a watery grave.

Brett Sabel (11)
Calder House School

MY KITTEN

My kitten is thin and tortoiseshell
She likes to play and ring a bell
Her tail is long and swishes about
Which makes me shout
She likes to purr
And has very soft fur
She likes to sleep
And cuddle down deep
She's awake all day
And loves to play.

Harry Oliver (8)
Calder House School

FIREWORKS

Fireworks go up with a surprise
They cry when they go
Up and up until - *bang!*
Then they get out the last one
All of a sudden
Whoosh! Whine! Crackle! Spit!
Whoosh! Whine! Crackle! Spit!
Goes the last explosion.

Jessica Rockey (11)
Calder House School

A STORMY DAY

It was very stormy,
The sea was getting grey.
The waves were crashing against the rocks,
The wind was very strong
And I was on the beach.

Sea-spray splashed on my face,
I tasted salt on my tongue.
I could hear water splashing and
The pebbles moved under my feet.
I felt cold and wet,
So I went home.

Thomas Robinson (10)
Calder House School

RAIN

She speaks softly,
She wears a long, white dress,
Which is silver-white silk.
Her hair is silken-soft,
She moves very quietly across the sky
And when she cries, her tears
Fall to the Earth,
When Rain speaks,
There's a whisper in the air.

Danielle Still (11)
Calder House School

LIGHTNING

His voice booms across the land,
Like drumbeats, deep and strong.
He is friends with Thunder, Wind and Rain.
When they get together and party,
They cause a storm.
He is a deadly thrower with his lightning spikes,
As he strides across the sky,
In his flashing silver armour.

Matthew Longshaw (10)
Calder House School

THE BEACH

There was yellow, golden sand,
It was a happy place,
A blue-green sea,
A clear, sunny day.
Seagulls crying, people calling,
Then the sky changed to grey.
Everybody's sad,
People pack up and go home.
The waves whack against the rocks,
A massive wind blows into shore,
It's not happy anymore.

Joshua Walford (8)
Calder House School

THE SEA

The sea is like a horse,
Half-green, half-grey,
Glistening and shining,
Hurtling forward
And clearing the cliffs.
Turning back
And flicking its tail,
With a swish and a splash,
As it gallops across the bay
And far away.

William Reynolds (8)
Calder House School

THE SEA

The water is grey on a stormy day,
Waves crashing against the rocks,
Fish swimming and darting in the sea.
Seagulls flapping their wings,
Seaweed floating on the water
And then the sea starts to calm.
It rises up, up, up into the air,
It's roaring with laughter,
As a huge wave breaks on the shore,
Bringing its treasures with it.
Shiny shells and glittering pebbles,
A wonderful sight to see.

James Dempster (8)
Calder House School

THE SEASIDE

The sea washes in sand and shells,
The fresh, salty smell goes up my nostrils,
Seaweed and sand,
Starfish,
Splashing in the rock pool,
Umbrellas stuck in the sand,
People sunbathing under them
On beach mats,
Boys and girls,
Splashing at the seaside.

Benedict Skipper (8)
Calder House School

FIREWORKS

Bang went the fireworks!
Whoosh went the Catherine wheel!
The flickering flames are dancing in the moonlight,
Whistling rockets go up and then
Explode!

Fairies dance in the night as
The children wave their sparklers
A screamer shoots up
It is a terrible noise!
I don't want to hear it again
And then it was time to go home.

Mary Nowell (11)
Calder House School

THE BEACH

A beautiful day at the beach,
The sea is shimmering and smooth.
Fish, shells and shrimps are in the rock pools.
The sea slams down on the shore,
With huge waves that are great to surf on.
As I sit, I hear a splash
And a massive swoosh.
The sky turns dark and
The day ends at the beach,
Until tomorrow.

Hayden Glinn (11)
Calder House School

WATER

She is a spirit,
Dancing as she moves,
With her popping bubbles
Swirling around her silken-blue gown.

She sounds like whales singing,
Her lovely song saying,
'Your water spirit is here.'
Her face is dyed in blue glitter,
Like bluebells with dew still on them.

But when she rises
In her pitiless rage,
She is as deadly as a comet.
Creating waves, higher than the cloudy sky,
But then she passes,
Leaving our world into her own.

Harriet Bailey (11)
Calder House School

GREEN

In spring trees turn green,
Slimy snakes slither up trees,
It makes me think of mint ice cream
And Christmas trees.
Green is the colour of football pitches
And long, green grass,
With a turtle snoozing!
Green is the colour of my classroom,
I like green!

Toby Cole (9)
Calder House School

CHRISTMAS IS FUN

Christmas is fun
When there are presents under Granny's tree
And we crawl round the back to see

Christmas is fun
As you hide in the snow
And throw snowballs

Christmas is fun
Because of Granny's Christmas pudding
Alight with surprises inside
Christmas is great!

Felix Fiducia-Brookes (9)
Calder House School

THE SEA

The waves are crashing on the cliffs
And clawing the rocks away,
Then bringing them in again.
The waves are enormous,
Crashing on the rocks.
Seagulls are squawking,
As the breakers pound down
On the sandy beach.
The grey clouds are full of rain,
The wind is howling like a wolf,
It's a very stormy day.

Joshua Charlesworth (8)
Calder House School

THE SEA

The sea swirls
Shimmering and shining,
The water is sparkling,
Little waves splashing,
Shimmering and shining.

Beautiful shells,
Glowing and glistening,
Little round pebbles,
Beautiful fish,
Glowing and glistening,
All of the secrets
Will one day be revealed.

Toby Wood (9)
Calder House School

THE SEA

The sea is rough and deadly,
Racing at the shore.
As fierce as a tiger,
Scraping its claws,
Scratching over the cliffs,
Finally catching its prey,
The tiger lies in the sun,
Sharing its treasures,
Shining shells and glistening pebbles
And then all is calm.

Alexander Lawrence (9)
Calder House School

THE COIN CUPBOARD

In my bedroom a cupboard stands,
Inside it I store elastic bands.

But the foreign coins are best,
I store them in an old vest.

I have some nice new Euro cents,
Which in England is only a few pence.

There's one from Bahrain, year 1902,
Some from UK, Jersey too.

Of course there's some from Ireland,
Not forgetting France.

In my bedroom a cupboard stands,
Where I store elastic bands!

Christy Blance (7)
Crockerton Primary School

I HAVE A SAFE

I have a safe to keep things in,
It's on top of my cupboard,
So people can't get in.
I hide my money in,
When I am in a hurry,
So I don't have to worry.
The safe is really high and out of harms way,
Until I need to play.
On a rainy day, I play shops
And pretend to buy a bunny that hops.

Emilea Whatley-Gibbs (7)
Crockerton Primary School

FAMILY PHOTO ALBUM

There's me
Sucking my imaginary dummy
But still in
Mum's tummy

Here's me again
With Bruce our rough collie
He couldn't walk
So he had a trolley

Here is me
Dressed at Christmas '93
A lovely horse I am

There's me again
Lovely me, wanting my tea.

Claudia Hickin (8)
Crockerton Primary School

WHALES

Whales swim, whales laugh,
Whales' favourite thing is a great big bath.
Whales have blubber and fat,
Which is not to be wondered at.
Whales eat krill and fish,
On one massive great big dish.
Whales swim round and round
And up and down,
With one big splashing sound.

Harry Baldwin (9)
Crockerton Primary School

DLP

Disneyland, a magical place
You're full of excitement
And you just can't wait
Then you see Belle in her glittering dress
And shout, 'I love Disneyland, it's the best!'

Along comes Woody with a snake in his boots
As it slithers up his leg
Meg and I shout, 'What a hoot!'
Walking down Main Street, we stop and stare
'This is magic!' we both declare.

Nick takes Mum to the castle and says,
'Will you marry me?'
Mum says, 'Yes'
Sean and Emily, my cousins are here
With eyes like saucers
They're full of good cheer
Here's to my auntie Del and uncle Ged
By nine o'clock they want their bed

Now on a roller coaster, up in space
Kyle beams with a smile on his face
If only we could stay here forever
Me, my friends and family together.

Rhiannon Daly (9)
Crockerton Primary School

ST GEORGE AND THE DRAGON

Galloping silver stallion,
Riding in the midnight gloom.
Human's eight-legged foe, spinning at its loom.
Dragon strides in moonlight blue,
A little clank of horse's shoe.

Maiden stands by dragon's side,
Dimming light like lapping tide,
Growing on the countryside,
Spear is drawn
And death is born.

Bee Lee (11)
Crockerton Primary School

WHY ME?

The bell rang, I lined up outside,
She graffitied the wall.
'It was here, Miss,' she lied.
I bowed my head, I closed my eyes,
I knew what was coming,
She always lies.

I followed the teacher with my head down low,
I hated her,
She had always been my foe.
Miss led me into the dark staffroom,
'I didn't do it.'
I swallowed and walked into doom.

I was given it, bad and hard,
The truth hidden
Inside my heart.
I stumbled out of the gloomy hole,
My head dropped low,
She had reached her goal.

Emily Jones (11)
Crockerton Primary School

FRIENDS

Friends are funky
groovy and cool.
We have some great times,
when we are at school.

We fiddle with our hair
and have lots of fun.
Playing outside in the
midday sun.

Friends are great,
trendy and kind.
Together we learn
and improve our minds.

We learn maths and English
and we sew and cook.
It's great to know,
we can share that look!

Lucy Gunter (9)
Crockerton Primary School

WHO AM I?

I am sleek
I am fast
I am the fisher of fishers
I can dive
I am brightly coloured
I am the king of the lake
I am the kingfisher.

James Scott Palmer (9)
Crockerton Primary School

WHO AM I?

I've got sharp teeth
I've got big claws
I've got short legs
Who am I?

The night has come
I like to come out
Hear my cries
Who am I?

My babies have come
The light has come back
I sink back into the water
Who am I?

I've got scaly skin
I've got a long tail
I've got small feet
Who am I?

A crocodile.

Felicity Webb (11)
Crockerton Primary School

WHO AM I?

I am big
I am slow
I have good sense of direction
I am blue
I have baleen in my mouth
I am the king of all whales
I am a blue whale.

Aaron Teager (9)
Crockerton Primary School

ST GEORGE AND THE DRAGON

I stole the red from the blaze in the fireplace
And placed it in the dragon's eye,
I took the green from a blade of grass
And placed it in the dragon's scales,
I took the anger from the fierce sky
And placed it in the dragon's soul.

I stole the gold from the phoenix's feather
And placed it on St George's spear,
I took silver from a bolt of lightning
And placed it in St George's armour,
I stole the strength from a young tiger
And placed it in St George's muscles.

I stole the black from an evil mind
And placed it in the swirling clouds,
I took the breath from a vampire bat
And placed it in the air;
The picture was finished.

George Baldwin (10)
Crockerton Primary School

A TALE OF A DRAGON

All I wanted was a peaceful walk
Then a man appeared through the sombre forest
He came with anger
I did not run
I tried to fight for my life
He speared me with a spear through my head
Blood drooled from my eye.

Curtis Saunders (9)
Crockerton Primary School

ST GEORGE'S QUEST

Echoes from the sombre forest,
Shadows that peer through trees
My horse full of interests
As I get closer, closer to the thing I dread
Dragon
The moon's beam of radiance ignites the sky
Black like charcoal, the night draws on
I steady my hefty steed
As white as a snowy owl in black night skies
Here I am
Waiting for the beast I fear
A deafening roar comes from a nearby cave
I wait, slowly, steadily, a strong, sturdy leg emerges
Next, the wide body of the dragon steps out proudly
In the cave, a fair maiden cries for help
I move forward, for a life is in danger
Then I see its teeth as sharp as icicles
Dripping with blood . . .

Alyssa Piper (10)
Crockerton Primary School

LION

Inside the lion's mane, the hot horizon,
Inside the hot horizon, the lion's skin,
Inside the lion's skin, a bushy tree,
Inside the bushy tree, the lion's prey,
Inside the lion's prey, a rushing river,
Inside the rushing river, the lion's foot,
Inside the lion's foot, a stony hill,
Inside the stony hill, the lion's mane.

Kristie Cockayne (10)
Crockerton Primary School

THAT WITTY, OLD HAMSTER

That witty, old hamster
Who lives in his cage,
His name is Stamper
And he chewed up this page.

He is like a big fur ball,
Running all around,
Running up the cage wall,
Without any sound.

When it is time to go to bed,
He hides in the paper,
He plays all night, until it's later,
Wearing his wheel out, until it's straighter.

In the end, he's quite a pain!
He's driving me up the wall,
I can't believe he's so annoying,
Because he's so small!

Felicity House (11)
Crockerton Primary School

WHO AM I?

A very long nose
And claws on my toes
And a big, bushy tail
Who am I?

Big, beady eyes
That is bothered by flies
And a big, bushy tail
Who am I?

Black and white stripes
That look like pipes
And a big, bushy tail
Who am I?

An anteater.

Christina Webb (11)
Crockerton Primary School

ST GEORGE

I rode to the cave,
My javelin in hand
And sword in scabbard.
I looked round, saw the scorched
Country and shuddered.
The dragon crept out,
I drew the stiletto from my
Sheath and let fly.
It pierced the dragon's front leg.
My horse charged,
The dragon snarled
And my horse reared.
I raised my javelin
And pierced the dragon's weakness,
The eye - a gateway
To a dark mind.
The scarlet blood
Scorched the ground.
The dragon was slain,
The battle won.
The maiden's token
Tied to my arm
And me a saint . . .

Joe Ramsden (9)
Crockerton Primary School

MY CHEST

I have a chest
Under my desk
It has a feather
And some treasure
It has two lolly sticks
And a wrapper off a Twix
I keep my diary inside it
And I have a doll beside it
I keep my pencil there
Next to it, I have a teddy bear
I have a chest
Under my desk
And oh, it is the best.

Sophie Minter (7)
Crockerton Primary School

DRAGON POEM

I could see a man
Striding through the forest,
With a sombre sky ahead,
I had the maiden tied to me,
I would not let her go.
Then I was speared,
Blood beaded out,
I had been stabbed.
With my large, scaly body
And my gigantic teeth,
I could not defend myself,
I was speared in the eye.

Sam Whatley-Gibbs (10)
Crockerton Primary School

ARSENAL

A rsenal are the best team
R eally I think they are
S urely you must think so
E very player is the best by far
N ever mind the other teams
A rsenal are the top
L eaving all the other teams to drop.

Jay Potter (9)
Crockerton Primary School

CHRISTMAS JOY

Christmas is a time for joy,
Presents for every girl and boy.
All are carol singing,
Church bells are loud and ringing,
But best of all is the Christmas lunch,
As we all sit round in a big, big bunch.

Hannah Manson (7)
Crockerton Primary School

THE SNAKE

S caly, slippery, slithery, slimy serpent.
N ostrils are set high on the head.
A dders are one species.
K illing is what they do to eat.
E ggs are what they lay to reproduce.

Georgina Henry (10)
Crockerton Primary School

FRUIT

I love fruit and it's good for you
Peaches, raspberries and blackcurrants too
Cherries so sweet
Pineapples we eat.

Plums are so soft, apples that crunch
Oranges so juicy, they're great to munch
Tomatoes so red and juicy and round
In autumn the blackberries are plentifully found.

Grapes hang in bunches, ready for picking
Lovely purple sloes, all ready for pricking
A nice, ripe banana looks tempting to me
Hanging in bunches in the top of a tree.

Oh, I'm so glad that fruit is good for me
But my favourite fruit has to be the kiwi
With its lovely green flesh and little black seeds
When I feel peckish, it's just what I need.

Siân Madge (9)
Crockerton Primary School

IN MY GARDEN

In my garden there is a mole,
He lives in a big black hole.
As blind as a bat
And as fat as a rat.
He pops his head up every night,
He gives me a big fright.

Jordan Henry (8)
Crockerton Primary School

In My Chest

I have a chest
Where I keep a Beanie called Jess
She has a friend called Bess
In the colourful chest

I have a lock
To lock them in
So they are kept
Deep within

I keep some jewels
In the chest
So I don't lose them
They're my party best.

Alexandra Muir (8)
Crockerton Primary School

My New Year's Resolutions

I will not throw the dog out the window,
I will look after my pets and not hurt them
And I will shut all the doors
I'll not moan at Mum's cooking
(Urgh! Fish again!)
I will never spit or shout or even stare
I will try my hardest and be helpful at school
And love my mum and dad and friends
I will go to bed when I am told
And go straight to sleep.

Robyn Harding (9)
Crockerton Primary School

TOM AND BUSTER

Buster is our pet dog,
Through the woods we daily trog,
He gets muddy paws and belly,
Comes straight home and watches telly.

He's mainly white with a few black spots,
He jumps and bites and barks a lot,
He's really good fun as my playmate,
Chasing, running about, until it's late.

Tom Lewis (7)
Crockerton Primary School

A DRAGON'S TALE

I saw him
His shiny armour pierced the night
His gallant steed strode through the forest
I froze with fear
I turned to ice
His razor-sharp spear was in the palm of his hand
As the moon died, so did I.

Nick Legg (9)
Crockerton Primary School

WHY?

When the vase gets broken, why do I always get the blame?
When the garden's untidy, why do I have to get the blame?
When the books get ripped, why do I always get the blame?
When someone breaks the pencil lead, why do I get the blame?
When the newspaper gets lost, why do I have to find it again?

Ben Clough (10)
Crockerton Primary School

THE PRELINGABLOBS

I met a family of insects
Called the Prelingablobs
And if you looked at them closely,
Their legs were covered in knobs.

I'd say they were about 2 inches tall,
They can be fat or thin,
Beware when they're around the water,
They might try to pull you in.

They went on a big adventure,
Through the garden fence,
I didn't dare to follow them,
The moment was very tense.

Right in front of them,
They saw a bumblebee,
It frightened them so very much,
They ran right up to me.

A moment or two later,
They saw a ladybird,
They were so very frightened,
That they didn't say a word.

They came across a centipede,
With lots and lots of legs
And each individual one of them,
Looked just like wooden pegs.

If I were a little Prelingablob,
I'm sure I'd like it a lot,
I'm not so sure about next-door's cat,
So actually, maybe not!

Siân Rowley (11)
Derry Hill CE Primary School

WHY?

Why do they worry me so much?
Make me feel I cannot touch.

Why are they so small and fit under my door?
Make me feel that they're keeping score.

Why do they scare me at night?
Make me call for someone to put on the light.

Why do I think about them before I go to sleep?
Makes me have nightmares about all the things that creep.

Why do I have to check under my bed?
Make sure there's nothing waiting to be fed.

Why do they make me scream and shout?
Makes my parents wonder what the trouble's all about.

Why do they nibble at my lunch?
Make me wonder what was that crunch.

Why do they attack me from the air?
Make me run for cover, that's just not fair.

Why do I have to check out my wellies?
Make sure they haven't left their own little smellies.

Why do others like to keep them as a pet?
Makes me realise they don't know that they're a threat.

Why don't they live quietly out of sight?
Makes me sure that they do it out of spite.

Why do I think they have a plan?
Make sure they take over the world from man.

Why are some so beautiful and graceful?
Makes me wonder why I feel so hateful.

Why? They are only bugs and insects I know,
But there is one crawling over my toe, *argh!*

Alice Nolan (11)
Derry Hill CE Primary School

THE MAGIC BOX
(Based on 'Magic Box' by Kit Wright)

I will put in the box . . .
The fantasy footballer taking a fabulous, fiery strike,
The fifth season on a summer night,
The swish of a silk sari on a black sun.
I will put in the box . . .
The majestic, marvel of a raging waterfall,
The sharp, slick freeze of the dainty icicle,
The smell of the burning embers as they crackle in an inferno.
I will put in the box . . .
The great, calm smile of an everlasting friendship,
The three gentle poses of a kind, loving mum,
The soft, smooth touch of a cuddly, caring teddy bear.
My box is fashioned from the greatest mathematician of all our age,
The clouds of danger from outer Venus
And bumpy palm tree bark from Paradise Island.

Hannah Massey (10)
Derry Hill CE Primary School

A LOVELY VOICE

A little ladybird with fluttering wings,
had a voice and with it she would sing.
All day and all night she'd not even yawn,
she would sing until the cock crowed at dawn.

She played a concert and everyone clapped,
she took a bow then went and napped.
All over the world people heard her sing
and what lovely joy it would surely bring.

Continents and nations became her stage,
kings, queens and presidents came too and paid.
They heard her sing sweet melodies
and were invited to another concert absolutely free!

The free concert was to be a special one,
where all the insect children came and enjoyed the fun.
She had an idea once the concert was done,
to start a singing academy for all the young.

She needed some help for she could not do it alone,
then thought of an old friend who taught her how to sing at home.
So she started her journey which was very, very far,
to speak to her teacher who lived in an old jam jar.

Her teacher who was a cricket named Mr Hop,
said he would help her 'til he dropped.
They sat and planned and set about,
a plan of which they did not doubt.

Very soon the academy was born,
it started in the early morn
and the beetles, caterpillars too,
all came to show what they could do.

So the little ladybird with her lovely voice,
brought together a family and everyone rejoiced.

Lauren Seager (10)
Derry Hill CE Primary School

SONG OF THE WITCHES

Bubble, bubble on the double,
Fire burn and cauldron bubble,
Wing of fly, claw of rat,
Foot of rabbit, tooth of cat,
Beady eye of feathered eagle,
Slime of slug, tail of beagle,
Shell of snail, spine of mole,
Beak of robin, far-off vole,
Tongue of hippo, cuckoo spit,
Mouth of frog and living nit,
Bubble, bubble on the double,
Fire burn and cauldron bubble,
Stir it, mix it, brew it well,
See it hiss, that's the spell.

Daisy Payne (11)
Derry Hill CE Primary School

MUM

'Is there going to be a war, Mum?
Bullets flying to and fro?
Will there be blood and pain, Mum?
Do we make a shelter down below?
Will our family stay together, Mum?
Will they bomb our home?
I feel unsure about the future, Mum,
I feel worried and alone.'

'My dear you're safe within my arms,
We will not hide away.
Don't fear bombs, air raid alarms,
Like it was in Grandma's day.
I'll keep your world here safe for you,
This family will not be apart
And English mums tell their children this too,
I can feel it in my heart.'

Naomi Jackson (10)
Forest & Sandridge Primary School

ANIMALS

Long ago the world was fine
There were beautiful trees, oak and pine
But now the happiness has ended
The beauty will never be mended
The fruit has been poisoned
The animals will die
Every time they see the rubbish
The animals sigh
They wish they'll never see rubbish again
But the animals don't know how and don't know when.

Hazel Travers (8)
Forest & Sandridge Primary School

THE STEPS UP THE CHIMNEY

The steps up the chimney,
One, two, three,
What can I see,
It's a magician's house,
I'm tiptoeing like a mouse,
I walk over to the chair,
He's as scary as a bear,
As I hide,
He begins to glide . . .

Natalie Bourne (10)
Forest & Sandridge Primary School

MY GUINEA PIG, SCRUFFY

I have a little guinea pig,
Scruffy is his name,
He is very loveable and very, very tame.
He likes to have a cuddle,
His little home is such a muddle.
His favourite food is carrots and hay,
He will be 4 years old in May.

Zoe Meakin (10)
Forest & Sandridge Primary School

A SMILE

A smile can bring a world of happiness.
It's hard to believe that a thing as small as that
Can bring so much joy to someone's life.
So next time someone you know is upset or down,
Just remember that that small gift is the best cure.

Jessica Dobson (10)
Forest & Sandridge Primary School

THE FUTURE

Will the future be dark or bright?
Will our children go off to fight?
To save our world, can this be right?
Our future seems so far away,
But it's getting closer every day.
Will our homes be in the sky
Or way deep down not way up high?
What does the future hold for us?
We really cannot say.
Just live our lives as best we can,
From day to day to day.

Richard Everett (10)
Forest & Sandridge Primary School

MY BROTHER

My brother's on Sky
He's trying to fly
I don't think he could
But he really, really should
My brother's in the circus
Trying to do flips
Whilst eating double dips
He slipped and fell
Down a well
'Yes, now he won't be silly,'
Said Mr and Mrs Gilly.

Dan Moore (10)
Forest & Sandridge Primary School

TITANIC

It was the day the Titanic set afloat,
The date was April, 1912.

Many people watched as the boat set sail,
The Titanic was a huge floating hotel,
It was known as the 'Unsinkable'.

The Titanic had only been at sea for 4 days,
It had hit an iceberg,
Down, down, down it went.

A lot of people died that dreadful night,
It was terrible,
The 'unsinkable' had sunk.

Rebecca Blackey (10)
Forest & Sandridge Primary School

THE STORM IS A DRAGON

The storm is a dragon
Stomping steadily through the creepy cave
Loud huffing
It stomps like thunder roars
Going madly
Banging his sharp claws
It's mad roar echoing
Echoing
Echoing
Echoing . . .

Daniel Hughes (9)
Freshbrook Primary School

THE STORM TIGER

The storm is the tiger
Prowling along its territory
Marking more each day
Lightning as an intruder
Dashes through the environment
The tiger rapidly kills its prey
Dead!

Andrew Nutt (10)
Freshbrook Primary School

A HORSE IS A LANDSLIDE

A horse is a landslide
Quaking through villages
Stampeding through anything in its way
Galloping down mountainsides
Eating through roads
Destroying wherever it goes
And most children ask, 'Where does it go?'

Lucas Gillett (9)
Freshbrook Primary School

LION STORM

The storm is a lion
Roaring through the noisy forest
Its dark, scary claws
Scaring every animal away
As it roars, a blizzard comes.
The storm is a lion
Howling.

Ka-Yan Cheung (8)
Freshbrook School

PEACOCK

The peacock is a rainbow
Clambering and jumping along the wet road.
The swift waving of the wing feathers
Of the gorgeous peacock squealing on its way.
She silently waddles as she grooms her feathers
With her soft tongue.
The colourful peacock is here.
The peacock is a rainbow.

Faye Millin (9)
Freshbrook School

FISH

With scales and skin so slimy
The fish's eyes so tiny
Swimming through the weeds all day
Carefully looking for its prey
Sweeping through the waters fast
Gazing as the fish go past
The little fish sleeps at last.

Rebecca Smyth (10)
Freshbrook Primary School

STORMY TIGER

The storm is a tiger,
Roaring in pain.
Hunting out for its prey.
Giant claps of thunder,
Rampaging on the dull pavements,
Out for revenge.

Priyanka Joshi (10)
Freshbrook Primary School

SNOW TIGER

Flakes fell down on the cold nose.
Running through the blizzard of the town.
Swiftly jumping like snow scattering the snowiest of snow.
Roaring as he prowls through the deep city snow.
As he roars, a blizzard comes.
The feeling of his snowy coat feels like the tickle of a flake falling.
Running through the blizzard leaving pattering footprints behind him.
The snow is the snow tiger.

Alexandra Lee (9)
Freshbrook Primary School

THE SUNNY BUTTERFLIES

The sun is a butterfly
Warping freely in the air
Springing her mellow wings
And drifting laboriously into calmness
Reflecting all her colours
Queen of all light
Dazzler of the sky
Like a glittery icicle
Because the sun is a butterfly.

Katie Stevens (10)
Freshbrook Primary School

STORMY ELEPHANT

A storm is an elephant
Stomping heavily.
Here and there, to and fro.
Booming around with
Deafening steps.

Lumbering across the country
Destroying everything in sight.
Dashing around wildly
With bone-chilling light that spreads
Like madness.

Carmen-Thea Harper (10)
Freshbrook Primary School

THE STORM

The storm is a tiger
Stomping along the icy alleyways
Its prey flying in different directions
Its claws prowling high in the blizzard air
Its skin flashing like stripes of lightning
Trees blowing, hitting every roof
Slate sliding, shattering as it hits the ground
The tiger's scared like a cat prowling
In the wind.

Megan Poppy (9)
Freshbrook Primary School

THE RAIN IS A WHALE

The rain is a whale
Paddling in and out the sea
Splashing through the icy waves
Hitting viciously every corner that's in sight
Lumbering solidly, as for the mammal's anger
The water mammal
Flooding.

Hannah Gale (10)
Freshbrook School

SUMMER

Swifting its hair up and down
As he jumps through the air making a soft sound
The faint sound of galloping
The quiet sound of gulping water
He who touches the soft, smooth skin
His beauty shining through the sun
As he is the only one who dares run
Through the summer sun
His soft voice of pattering sunshine
He is the colour of daffodils
A fiery eye
Hibernates through the winter.

Josh McHugh (8)
Freshbrook School

SNOW TIGER

The snow is a tiger
Its tail is like the wind blowing.
The snow is a tiger
It roars when it gets angry.
The snow is a tiger
Falling from the body of the tiger
Launching through the snow
The sabre tooth cries.
The snow is a tiger.

Joe Shepherd (9)
Freshbrook School

THE SUN IS A BUTTERFLY

The sun is a butterfly,
Fluttering around the world,
Bringing warmness to cold places,
Beating its wings.
The small butterfly, the colour of the sun,
Brings happiness to people that are cold-hearted,
Still flying and making things grow.
The tiny butterfly, straining to keep in the air,
Making love stick in mean people's hearts,
Keeping peace on Earth,
Like kind people try to do.

Chloe Roberts (9)
Freshbrook Primary School

THE SUN

The sun is a butterfly
Swaying past the wind
Shining bright through the air
Glittery colours like you've never seen
High up in the sky
The sun and butterfly lies
Floating through the clouds
Moving like a cat's tail
Fluttering past the birds
The sun is a butterfly.

Gemma Louise Scott (8)
Freshbrook School

Snow Leopard

Its gleaming eyes sparkling in the sunlight
Pouncing on its prey
It comes over the shining mountains
Its fluffy soft coat keeping him warm
The breezy wind whistling over the mountains
Claws digging into the penguin's heart
Tasting the fresh blood that's pouring out
And chasing the others into the freezing *cold water*
And watching the snow leopard stride
Away waiting for the right time
To come out.

Jamie McDougall (10)
Heytesbury Primary School

Sunset

The magical light of the roasting sun,
Blowing out warmth like a heater,
Lights up the countries like a lamp to an ant,
Falling slowly like a meteor flying past Earth.
The heat of an oversized oven,
Drying up all the wet soggy water on the ground.
Neither freezing nor cold, nor snow nor rain,
            but it's sunny!

Nathan Bond (10)
Heytesbury Primary School

Winter Poem

Donna, I think she's three or four
Oh, I'm not really sure
No one's awake just me and my mate
Now I can hardly wait
All of my presents might come in a crate.

Holly berries are red
Old socks under the bed
Lights are turned off
Lonely children cough
Young puppies bark.

Jessica Agate (8)
Heytesbury Primary School

BEAR

Blood thirsty creature ready for prey,
Carnivorous mammal with razor-sharp teeth.
Supreme hunters built like tanks,
Rustling through the grass.
Claws digging into rich soil.
Aggressive attitude towards its slab of meat
A bear with a selfish way.
If any animals trespass the bear's territory
Roar! Roar! Roar!

Liam Beattie (11)
Heytesbury Primary School

FROST

The white elegant blanket covering the cars,
The white freckled bits of snow gleaming,
Twinkling in the eyes of the sun.
A mini version of a snowstorm.
The white blanket mollifying in the orange ball of fire
Slowly evaporating,
Slowly disappearing.
The elegant blanket vanished,
Frost!

Scott Lewis (10)
Heytesbury Primary School

SUNSET

Pretty gloom, sunlight pink,
Alarming red, greying blue,
Alarming yellow, rainbow orange, carrot orange.
Heaven's calling, 'Goodnight!'
Devils stalking

Daylight wonder, lilac blue.
Goodnight sunlight,
Good day moon.

Chickens roost,
Flowers close,
Faint stars mellow yellow,
Sun comes running, moon comes running at you.

Sunset safari, people coming
Sapphire blue skies,
People late, big disgrace.
Satin skies,
Seen a sunset, have you?

Rebecca Newman (9)
Heytesbury Primary School

A COP

A brain like a computer.
The radio echoing in the background.
Armour like a bull.
Ready to bulldoze the door down.
The house surrounded by giant weapons ready to do its work.
The black and silver gun lays in the brown silky holster.
Ready to pull out and hit the trigger . . .

Ben Agate (10)
Heytesbury Primary School

A TABLE

It stands on four legs,
Doesn't move at all.
Used as a desk,
Used for a stall.

Varnished wooden surface,
Blue, blue feet.
Polished underbelly,
Tucked into it a seat.

A place where you can sit,
A place where you can lay.
Legs made of steel,
It sleeps all day!

Arms made of plastic,
A grey wooden head.
Because it's flat and smooth,
It's perfect for a bed.

Pencil on its back,
Ruler on its arm.
Because it can't move,
It can't do any harm.

Daniel Bone (10)
Heytesbury Primary School

THE LEOPARD

Razor-sharp paws,
Very fit like a man.
Fast like a tiger.
Black spots and white,
Hiding in the snow.

Sasha Bowen (9)
Heytesbury Primary School

PENGUIN

This tiny but mighty fellow fights
For a living and for babies.
This gentle slither loves to toboggan
Into the sea and watch
All the seals as they go past.

This agile swimmer jumps
In with a loopety-loop
The streamlined black and white figure swims away, penguin!
Off on a hunt to get some food
To regurgitate for young. Sardines

Zoom, whizz and swish
Off home back to bed,
But babies want food . . .

Heather Newman (9)
Heytesbury Primary School

FROST

The green grass glimmering with the sun,
Water droplets *plop* off roofs.
White frost covers the freezing scenery.
Not a speck of green across the whole crystal floor.

Green at the bottom,
White at the top,
Creatures freeze,
Below minus levels
Of the winter garden.

Thomas Dalby (9)
Heytesbury Primary School

THE GREAT WHITE

As the shark stalks the prey,
Timing it just right to kill the seal on impact,
Ripping through the flesh like a beast,
The scent of running blood attracting other
        beasts of the sea,
As the size of a minibus it dwarfs the seals,
As the dead carcass of the seal floats to the surface,
Its huge razor-sharp teeth tear at the meat,
As it devours the carcass bite by bite,
With its lethal weapons,
And its powerful body,
The shark is top predator of the sea,
It is an animal that can't be named or tamed.

Alex Merx (10)
Heytesbury Primary School

SUNSET

Orange fire-blazing sun,
Scorching brightly,
Sky scattered with exotic blues and warming reds.
Hills glistening with the bedtime sun.
Sunlight park,
Owl's dawn,
Fox's teatime,
See the light, miniature tint of beaming orange,
Sinks down over the hills.
Everywhere darkening for the long, blustery night.
Stars start to appear twinkling brightly.
The sun falls asleep down the lush, dark green, grassy hills.

Emily Whitcombe (9)
Heytesbury Primary School

THE KANGAROO

A red coated fur with orange sunlight tint
All velvety and soft with a surely silky touch.
Swaying through the wild wind grass
With a sunset straight ahead.

A great trampoline springing about
With lightning boisterous powerful kicks.
Muscular shoulders in a galloping motion
A baby joey wobbles inside.

Eyes dazed like a sunlight spark
Elegant looks on its long pale face.
Mountainous ears like chilly breeze mittens
An elasticated tail like the great baboons.

Sharp finger nails like a miniature dagger
Bony stick legs with large thumping feet
There he goes ten feet in the air.

Samantha Grindley (11)
Heytesbury Primary School

WINTER POEM

S   now falls down all the time
N   owadays it's not a crime.
O   ur home all white and snowy
W ithout our tree so shiny.

S   anta will soon be here
A   nd his sleigh is pulled by reindeer.
N   aughty children staying up late.
T   onight I'm playing with my mate.
A   nd tomorrow I will see my fate.

Emma Reade (9)
Heytesbury Primary School

WINTER POEM

T hrowing snowballs in the sky
R ound the corner up high
E at the crumble
E at the pie to keep you warm at night.

S anta is coming to the boys and girls
T o give them all some presents
O h the girls have pearls
C an the boys have pheasants?
K icking the snow up in the air
I see the snowman wave
N ow if you look out of the window, you'll see the snowman
G o out to the garden and make an angel
S anta is coming I hope you have fun.

Molly Stuart (8)
Heytesbury Primary School

WINTER POEM

T ree tops full of snow
R ed-breasted robins on the go
E verybody having fun
E verybody on the run.

H olly berries as red as can be
O ld people knitting something for me
L ike it now so you can be seen
L ovely jumpers knitted green
Y ou won't need one just come to me.

Lauren Pinnell (9)
Heytesbury Primary School

FROST

As the sun glints through rigged crevices,
The titanic clouds arrange themselves
Into the shape of a fierce giant.
The thick misty air transforms the sunlight,
Very dim . . .
Trees white with frost,
Like they've been sprinkled with pure white flour.
Icicles droop off lonely houses.
The grass sparkles like crystals
That catch the light every single second.
Jack Frost has made our gardens and fields.
A magnificent wonderland!

Caitlin Skeates (11)
Heytesbury Primary School

AUTUMN FALLS

Autumn leaves are falling,
Scarlet-red, copper-red, rusty-red.
There are colours forming in the sky.
Animals begin to hibernate
In their warm, toasty homes,
The trees are bare and sad,
Yet, there are beautiful colours around them.
They form an ant hill-like pile.
While children play with the leaves
The arms of the trees reach out
As if they want to play too.
The gold, brown leaves are telling us,
'Don't rip us up! We want to play too!'

Florence Corp (11)
Kingsbury Hill House School

A RAGING WAR

A young demon sat on the Bayside,
Cast his eyes on the swirling tide.
And then he saw it
A dark shape moving to the West,
A ship of doom, the best of best.
He has returned.
He ran to the palace of Skaerioor
Told of what to come, returning gloom
A raging war
The King's army moved on West,
They waited, patient, to challenge the best.
And then they came
A vicious horde, as black as night
The two sides charged and began the fight
The King looked up through spear and sword
Turned his head to the advancing horde.
His men were slaughtered, everywhere,
He was the last one left, the last one there.
He knew alone he had no chance,
He needed help and help came fast.
Prince Firen, Lord of the North,
Came on his ship with his gigantic horde.
His blue eyes shone into the night,
He and his horde carried on the fight.
He cried, 'So many have you slain.
I swear you shall never see daylight again!'
They gained victory.
The horde they moved back to the East,
And in the palace they held a feast.

Once again, the whole of evil breaking through,
        good has been sealed.

Matthew Dyas (9)
Kingsbury Hill House School

IS IT AUTUMN?

Suddenly I feel a cold wind roar up my spine,
Then a nutmeg leaf swirls to the hard ground;
It is autumn.

As I walk past a garden I smell a bonfire.
As I look around me, the trees, they are all bare;
It is autumn.

The days seem to grow dark too quickly for me to
Catch them as I walk through the ghostly mist;
It is autumn.

My eyes spot a fruit tree with no fruit.
I stare at the cold frosty ground;
They are all down there.

A little animal grabs its food, pulls it in and hurries off home.
As I walk home in the door I feel a warm fire.
Now I know that it is autumn.

Victoria Bushell (10)
Kingsbury Hill House School

AUTUMN DAYS

It's a cool, crisp morning,
Fields are like muddy lakes
Because of last night's rain.
Mountains of golden-brown and
Chestnut-coloured leaves surrounding the tree.
The whistling wind swirls the leaves into wonderful patterns.
Mum said the lazy November winds chilled her to the bone.
But I'm inside by a nice warm fire.

Poonam Mandalia (10)
Kingsbury Hill House School

THE ORCHESTRA OF AUTUMN

The leaves painting the ground as a copper brass carpet.
The smell of dampened leaves and moss
As cascades of water pound on the leaves' bare backs.
A ravenous pack of wolves charging at the branches
For the leaves to descend.
The sun fading behind a curtain of moulting leaves.

The orchestra of the dying sounds of summer
Fading into a mercilessly wet, cold season.
The crackling fire of leaves, crunching as they are trodden upon.
The howl of wind slipping through branches of helpless trees
And children gathering the last of conkers
In the shadows of the collapsing breeze of autumn.

Philippe Clayton (11)
Kingsbury Hill House School

ALL ABOUT AUTUMN

The dropping of scarlet leaves is like music to my ears.
The howling wind sounds like a wolf bellowing at the moon.

The leaves on the tree turn red like my rosy cheeks.
My warm breath against the cold wind enables me to make smoke.

Animals get ready to hibernate for their long winter sleep.
I wrap up warm with layers of thick, warm and soft jumpers.

Outside in the thrilling cold, hands unable to fasten buttons.
With your very sharp axe cutting the firewood

The clock stops like a statue and days get shorter.
The tree rattles on my window and the howling fades away.

Kishan Patel (11)
Kingsbury Hill House School

AUTUMNUS SENSUS

You wake up to early morning white frosts
And smell the wood smoke in the breeze
Of the autumn wind.

You go out in the frozen winds
Dead sound from the summer before,
And feel the damp textured wood
From the fire that was left out that night.

The parks are frozen by the death of summer
You kick cinnamon-red, rusty-brown and
Banana-yellow leaves on the paths
The gardeners make Himalayas of leaves.

After the cosy lie-ins of the morning
Everybody warms in front of the blazing fires
In the peaty night.

Tristan Cotterill (11)
Kingsbury Hill House School

THE MEETING

Trees hustle and bustle in front of the moonlight,
Footsteps crack twigs on the ground,
Ivy crawls down my neck; what an evil spirit.
My arms are long and thin,
People disturb me when I sleep.

Eyes of a girl in mine.
I saw tears run down her face.
Eyes are closed but I can still see her.
I tried to comfort her,
But realised I am only a tree.

Magella Oldcorn (10)
Kingsbury Hill House School

AUTUMN

I wake up and find the leaves on the trees
Look like fire on the hearth.
I open my windows and see armies of pheasants
Marching through other people's gardens.

I open my door and step outside onto grass
That looks like millions of crystals.
The leaves are fiery-orange,
Golden-yellow flames.

When I walk through the forests,
I smell the strong fragrance of nuts and soil.
A smell so strong I can almost taste it.

Walking back through the forest,
The sunset looks like a fat tangerine.
Later, beautiful fireworks light up the night sky
And spooky pumpkin faces glare through windows.

Ella Cochran-Patrick (10)
Kingsbury Hill House School

SPITFIRE

Spitfire going around flying high
Flying high in the sky.
Shooting down the German planes
Shooting them while it rains.
The German tanks trampled the Cliffs of Dover
They trampled them and they went right over.
But my spitfire was still flying high
Flying high in the sky.

Christopher Dyas (8)
Kingsbury Hill House School

AUTUMN TREES

The wind whistles loud and low,
Trees bed with the strains,
The trees grow bare with exhaustion.

The wind blows cold.
Fat leaves, thin leaves
Bristle on the floor.
Apples from the orchard
Tumble from their trees.

The trees are howling like wolves
Which are hungry for their food.
Condensation on every breath:
Hallowe'en ghosts trying
To escape from our mouths.

Philip Williams (10)
Kingsbury Hill House School

BLACK BEAUTY

The drumming of her hooves across
The rocky land.
Her tail waving in the wind.
And her mane waving in the air
As she gallops along.
She is a man's best friend.
Her coat is as black as night.
She is as fast as lightning,
And as she gallops through the night
She will jump all the rivers
And race all the birds.

Patricia Grove (10)
Kingsbury Hill House School

MY OLDER SISTER

My older sister's thirteen,
She goes to boarding school.
She's weird but she's not mean,
She sometimes acts like a fool!

She's very funny and
She can be really kind,
When she's ill she has lemon and honey but
She really doesn't mind.

Wycombe Abbey's where she goes,
But she'll be my sister forever,
She could be an alien no one knows,
Or even a Cyclops . . . Never!

Sonali Patel (10)
Kingsbury Hill House School

LORD OF THE RINGS

Warriors get ready
Archers get steady.
They got out their bows
They lined up in rows.
Children had to fight
Their weapons were light.
The enemy came
Fierce and untame.
Legolas got to the front
There was the sound of a hunt.
Legolas shot an arrow
It hit the enemy straight from the bow.

Nicholas Dawes (8)
Kingsbury Hill House School

ANIMALS

I love puppies they are cute,
If they bite me I call them a brute.
Cats are nice, they are sweet,
They walk about by your feet.
I adore mice they are great,
They run so fast you'll be too late.
Horses are playful they are so fun,
If they gallop it's their run.
Monkeys swing high and monkeys swing low,
If you get too close just watch them go.
Foxes are sly, they creep around,
Sometimes they can be orangey-brown.
Birds fly around in the sky,
As they go from low to high!

Ciara Connell (8)
Kingsbury Hill House School

MY TREE

There was a tree in my garden
I used to always climb it
It was in my orchard
That means it was an apple tree.
It was very tall, so I needed a chair
It was very wide and easy to climb
Until a big storm came.
Thunder and lightning crashed at it
Winds blew it from side to side
Pushing and hurting it
Then, silence! It stopped.
Our tree was on the ground.
Part of my life gone.

Kit Williams (8)
Kingsbury Hill House School

THE GREAT HILL

A hill named Kon,
Named by Sir John,
It is so, so high,
And a great place to lie,
Gazing up at the sun.

The name may be wild,
That Sir John and his child,
Would think of every day,
Especially sunny, warm days,
Gazing up at the sun.

The village up there,
Has flowers so rare,
And logs in piles,
And a farmer called Giles,
Gazing up at the sun.

The hill named Kon,
Named by Sir John,
It is beautifully wide,
And sits next to the Tide,
Gazing up at the sun.

The hill by the sea,
Makes everyone full of glee,
The excellent ledges,
In snow you need sledges!
To view the great views in one;
Gazing up at the sun.

Thomas Dawes (10)
Kingsbury Hill House School

SUMMER

Summer is hot.
Summer has flowers, grass and trees.
Everything is big and green.
Trees are full of leaves.
The grass is green and daffodils and poppies grow.

Summer has men cutting the grass.
Children go to the sea and make castles.
Summer has flowers of bright colours.
That is summer.

Richard Martin-Barton (8)
Kingsbury Hill House School

FLOWERS

F   lowers are nice
L   ots of very nice colours they can be,
O   f them all I like the lily
W   ater them or they will die
E   ars they have some people say
R   oses smell very nice in the day,
S   nowdrops come out in spring

I think they are nice.

Rebecca Drew (9)
Kingsbury Hill House School

THE PIG

I've got a pig living in my house,
Worst of all, he's related to me,
He eats too much food but that's not all,
He wastes electricity.

His name is Bob, and he never cares,
When he knocks over tables and chairs,
But probably worse, my mum is his mother,
You see this pig, is actually my brother!

Hannah Hollis (9)
Kingsbury Hill House School

BEST FRIENDS

I have to tidy up my house.
I even have to clean my mouse.
I've got to tidy up my room,
So I'll use my dusty broom.
You're wondering why this I say,
It's because my friend's coming over today.
I've got to keep my whole house tidy,
Because today's the big day, today is Friday.

Abigail Bullock (9)
Kingsbury Hill House School

MONKEYS

I like monkeys
They're very sweet
They eat bananas, pears and meat.
Monkeys come in different shapes and sizes
Apes, gorillas and chimps to surprise us!
Monkeys sleep high in the trees
And pick at one another's fleas.

Freddie Corp (8)
Kingsbury Hill House School

MY GERBILS

One is called Nibbles
And the other Snowy,
Nibbles is brown and has
Cute black eyes.
Snowy is grey and white.
They squabble and squeak
Throughout the day.
They nibble on kitchen rolls
Until they are tired
And sleep through the night
In a bundle of hay.
Now it's the end of my poem.
The gerbils start over again.

Alex Hill (9)
Kingsbury Hill House School

BONFIRE NIGHT

B   lazing, burning, bangs.
O   range, odour, observe.
N   oisy, November, night.
F   irework, flames, flicker.
I   rritating, ignite.
R   owdiness, red.
E   xcitement, explosive, extinguish.

N   uisance.
I   ndigo.
G   low, gunpowder, Guy Fawkes.
H   ot dogs, hot chocolate, heat.
T   orch, timber, taper.

Samantha Ockwell (10)
Kingsbury Hill House School

MY GRANNY KITE

My kite is not a big kite
I call it my granny kite
A gift from you know who
With colours of the rainbow
It lights up a cloud or two

My kite seems to come alive
As soon as it catches the wind
Soaring high and pulling on its string

Flying high in the sky
I'm sure my kite is saying thank you
After all kite doesn't want to be a wallflower
Leant against the side of my bedroom wall
On a fine windy day.

Sophie Mattick (9)
Kingsbury Hill House School

TITANIC

She is sailing on the ocean,
Cold but far away,
Joyful, smiley people
Laughing all day,
While Jack was getting tied up
Rose was drinking out of a cup,
Suddenly she hit something,
Hard and strong
Rose began to sing a song.

If you haven't yet guessed,
What this might be,
Take a trip to the far away deep blue sea

Kirsty Tyler (9)
Langley Fitzurse CE Primary School

USELESS

I am
The old teddy bear
High in the loft
The yellow mouldy banana
Gone all soft
The blind
That won't close

I am
The ripped homework sheet
Floating in sewage
The rotten school book
With a missing page
The ruler snapped in two

I am
The sharpener
That never gets emptied
The fighting robot
That never got made
The tapestry
Broken in bits

I am nothing too special
Nothing too good
So leave me alone like you should . . .

Maddy Dann (10)
Langley Fitzurse CE Primary School

I WISH

If I had magic powers,
I would not have to take any showers.
I could fly up to the moon,
Drive a racing car all afternoon.

Eat as much chocolate as I'd like,
Ride the mountains on my bike.
Buy a million PlayStation games,
Ride with Santa, hold the reins.
I wish . . . I wish!

Alexis Wormald (11)
Langley Fitzurse CE Primary School

NO ONE SPECIAL

I am a sheep
That is never sheared

I am a ball
That never gets kicked

I am the hair
That never gets brushed

I am the light
That is never used

I am the horse
That is never rode

I am the voice
That never speaks

I am the fan
That is never cool

I am the pool
That is never touched

I am nothing, nobody, no one special at all!

Jessica Fairbairn (9)
Langley Fitzurse CE Primary School

WARHAMMER ACROSTIC

G oblins attack
A rmed with spears.
M arauding Orcs.
E mpire defends their Elector Count.
S ldiers slayed on the floor.
W ar is deadly,
O rcs scream savagely
R anks wait silently till,
K arl Franz
S houts, 'Charge'.
H ordes of men charge,
O rcs lay fearlessly with
P oled spears in their hearts.

W here the battle rages on,
A rtillery fires.
R eiksguard charge on their
H orses.
A rms swipe with swords.
M asses of Orcs plunder and pillage,
M urdering the Empire.
E ntire regiments blow Orcs to pieces,
R eiksguard are alive.

E mpire fight the
M enacing Orcs.
P istoller shoots.
I t kills Goblins.
R avaging Militia
E ventually win the tragic battle.

Dewi Evans (9)
Langley Fitzurse CE Primary School

AT SCHOOL

Coming down for breakfast,
Fiddling with my hair,
I will be late for school,
I don't care

Back in the classroom,
Back to the work,
Sit on the carpet
Without a jerk.

Sit at your tables,
It's nearly lunch,
Make sure you
have a good munch.

After your play time,
Got to calm down,
In other words don't,
Make a sound.

Sit in your art seats,
Draw very neat,
Picture something nice,
You could eat.

Push back the table,
Get in to a circle,
Pick your favourite toy,
It's got to be purple.

Tidy your tables,
Time to go home,
Sit down quietly,
And don't moan!

Sophie Chalmers (9)
Langley Fitzurse CE Primary School

A DAY AT THE SEASIDE

The seaside is sandy,
You eat lots of candy,
The seaside is warm,
You will like popcorn,
Ditch the meat and
Eat lots of sweets,
You lie on the sunbed
And get very red,
The next thing I know,
We have got to go,
Look a rockpool!
It looks cool!
I've found a crab.
Oh no! There's our cab.

Victoria Seales (10)
Langley Fitzurse CE Primary School

THE BEACH

T   he beach is a place full of cheer,
W   here him and her never disappear
E   verybody has lots of fun.

B   est of all in the lukewarm sun.
E   very day when the tide comes in,
A   ll the people laugh and sing
C   heerful faces everywhere,
H   appy days at the beach were there.

Miriam Stiglitz (10)
Langley Fitzurse CE Primary School

UNHAPPY I AMS

I am,
The match never
Been struck,
The piece of wood,
Never been cut,
The old, tatty shirt
That nobody wears.

I am,
The puppet
With no strings,
The pen that
Is broken into ten things
The runt,
That will never quite fit.

I am,
The ink that always rubs off,
The dolphin
With the really bad cough,
The tormented dog
Which never gets fed.

I am unique
I look like a freak,
I'm nothing
Nobody special.

Mike Flynn (10)
Langley Fitzurse CE Primary School

SOCCER SAD, I AMS

I am a Liverpool player,
That's always on the bench.
The football,
That's hidden in the trench.

I am the pitch,
Which doesn't get used.
A few,
Spotlights that have blown a fuse.

I am the football goal,
That's tattered and torn
And the opposite field
That is made out of corn.

Chenise Austin (9)
Langley Fitzurse CE Primary School

MY FRIENDS

Kez is sporty, sometimes naughty,
Shannon's tall and very cool,
Alexis is very funny, sometimes she thinks about her tummy
Mimi is very girly, she wishes that her hair was curly
Rach is very speedy and she is really cheeky.

Now you know all my friends
Our friendship will never end
Wait a minute then you'll see
A little something about me.

My name is Amy and I'm very crazy
I love my friends in every way.

Amy Stutt
Langley Fitzurse CE Primary School

ELEPHANT

E   lephants are big and grey,
L   eaping elephants are usually rare,
E   ating all day, sleeping all night,
P   icking the fruit from the treetops,
H   elping their young feed,
A   nd protecting them from danger,
N   ever mess with an elephant,
T   heir tusks are rather sharp!

Chantelle Chapman (10)
Langley Fitzurse CE Primary School

WHEN CATS CHASE MICE

Cats chase mice
Because they're nice.
They chase them and
They race
And if to say
Cats are gentle
I think they are mental.

Peter Drake (7)
La Retraite Swan

CAT, BAT, MOUSE

My cat met a bat,
Who met a mouse,
Who met a louse,
And they lived in a house,
That's that.

James Cole (7)
La Retraite Swan

THE CAT AND THE DOG

The cat tries to get the fish
He has a little dish
The cat wakes the dog
And then gets caught
I shall not go there again
He thought.

Thomas Newman (8)
La Retraite Swan

SCHOOL!

The sun is shining
The clouds are showing,
It's raining, pouring
Teachers blubbering,
Getting boring
Nearly sleeping,
It's raining, pouring
Door is opening,
Teacher coming
Test approaching,
People moaning
Heart is bumping,
Someone groaning
It's raining, pouring
Pen is wobbling
Sweat is pouring
Now it's thunder and lightning.

Jacob Simpkins (9)
Luckington Community School

WHO AM I?

I'm small and I squeak
And if I see a cat I don't peak.
Cheese is what I eat.
My fur is lovely and neat.
I have a huge long tail
And if you stand on it I bite or I wail.
I've got sharp teeth
And in the wild I might live on a leaf.
I don't normally live in a house.
So what am I?
An elephant,
No silly! A mouse!

Rebecca Thompson (10)
Luckington Community School

SEASONS

Spring is showery, flowers blossoming
And pretty primroses.

Summer is hot and brings cooling showers,
Apricots and gilly flowers.

Autumn is fresh and dull
Then the pheasants come out.

Winter is nippy, brings sleet
And blazing fires.

Kathryn Hutchinson (11)
Luckington Community School

Colours Of The Rainbow

What is brown? A tree trunk is brown
in its midnight gown.

What is blonde? Your hair is blonde
swishing in the air.

What is white? The moon is white
in the silent night.

Jake Beckett (7)
Luckington Community School

Outside A Chair

Outside a chair is a room
Outside a room is a hall
Outside a hall is the countryside
Outside the countryside is a city
Outside a city is the world
Outside the world is space
Outside space is the universe.

Elizabeth Hutchinson (11)
Luckington Community School

The Bad Nightmare

A blood-curdling scream cuts through the air,
A werewolf howls deep in its lair,
A vampire sucks blood galore,
But it wants more and more.

Lightning flashes round my house,
Nothing is as quiet as a mouse.
Everything is scary tonight,
Everybody will get a fright!

Caroline Kyle (9)
Luckington Community School

MAD BOY

M ad boy.
A   mad boy in the class.
D   riving Miss Hagley up the wall.

B   eing a pain.
O   h no! He's throwing pens,
Y   ucky smell.

Harrison Moore (9)
Luckington Community School

SPIDERS

Spooky
Crawling in my bed
Weaving on me
I opened one eye
Loads of spiders
On my head
Tickling me
Everywhere.

Jamie Jobbins (8)
Luckington Community School

WINDOW CAT

W indow cat staring into space
I sit on the window sill still as can be
N o one knows I'm here
D oors are creaking my bones are shaking
O n my own in the house
W indow cat is lurking round the house.

C an you see me?
A gain I wander round the house
T rying to find my supper.

Jennifer Baron (10)
Luckington Community School

THE CREAKY DOOR

The door opens, it creaks
I turn to see
A dark shadow looking for blood
I can't seem to run
I'm stuck standing to the ground
He comes closer
I scream, *'Argh!'*
He comes closer again
Bites his way into my neck
A piece of blood drips on the ground.
            'Argh!'

Abigail Boulton (9)
Luckington Community School

MANCHESTER UNITED

M um let's watch Man U are playing
A nd they're winning
N aughty Seaman
C heer for the crowds
H elp Beckham
E ast wing coming
S uper heroes score
T ricky goalkeeper
E arning the ball
R olling in the goal.

U nited have won
N il to Arsenal
I n Old Trafford
T en goals to Man U
E verton next week
D o the goals Becks in training.

Liam Dowker (9)
Luckington Community School

SKELETONS

S keletons are made,
K ill people in their cosy bed,
E at their slimy liver and guts,
L ike living underground in the dirt,
E vil comes and never ends,
T hen life or death drowned alive,
O nly a silver dagger hurts a skeleton,
N obody knows how to kill it.

Alex Arnault-Ham (10)
Luckington Community School

PETS

P retty poodles are so sweet.
E very day they like to eat.
T arantulas and reptiles aren't so nice.
S ome people even keep rats and mice.

Jeffrey Charles Simpkins (10)
Luckington Community School

THE LOVELY GARDEN

Roses are red,
With a lovely scent.
It was the most beautiful place,
I ever went.
The rain trickles down my face,
It hardly ever ruins the place.
The trees are bright green,
The freshest they've ever been.

Nathan Johnson (8)
Nythe Primary School

MY TEDDY

My teddy's name is Pooh Bear,
He sleeps with me every night,
He is so warm and cuddly
And doesn't even bite
And when I hug him closely,
He gives a little sigh
And snuggles up beside me
And winks his little eye.

Rebecca Ferguson (8)
Nythe Primary School

THE SECRET

I've lost it.
Where is it?
I've lost a secret.
Where could it be?
Oh where could it be?
Where is the secret . . . I told?

Is it under the table?
Under the chair?
Under a pillow?
I don't know where.
Is it under the sofa?
Under a plant?
What is that secret I told?

I still can't find it.
I can't think where it's gone.
That secret,
I told.
It's somewhere else,
Vanished,
In another world,
Not here,
Not anywhere!

I guess I'll never find it now,
I'm going to burst into tears.
I'm feeling really guilty,
I feel like saying sorry,
But I can't find the courage.

I've lost that secret for ever.

Toni Collins (8)
Nythe Primary School

CUTHBERT

My bear called Cuthbert
Is my best friend
He may be a bear but he's wise
And protects me day and night

Cuthbert's always there when
I'm happy or sad,
He makes me feel good
And stops bad dreams
From coming this way.

I love my best friend Cuthbert
He's the oldest one.
I love him the most
And always will.

Talitha Cogan-Stevens (6)
Nythe Primary School

MAGIC

Magic rabbits in a box,
Secret trunks with keys and locks,
Coloured marbles can pass,
Underneath an upturned glass,
Card with jacks,
Hats in black,
Silver coins which disappear.
Abracadabra, never fear
Short string, long string,
Magic is my favourite thing.

Luke Oakey (9)
Nythe Primary School

DINOSAURS

'There's something in the playground Miss!
It's something that roars!
There's something on the roof top Miss!
It might be dinosaurs!'

'It's fantasy dear, just fantasy!
We know dinosaurs weren't here to stay
I can tell you ever so truthfully,
They've all gone away!'

'But what were those shadows,
In such scary shapes?'
'It's hedges dear, just hedges,
They're being pruned today.'

'But what are those things right over there,
Those things with gaping mouths?
Those things with fearsome roars?
Those things that step on buildings Miss?'

C R A S H !

'It's those dinosaurs!'

Gillian Langston
Nythe Primary School

HULLABALOO!

I like my holiday
In the sun
Because it's fun
And I played with Sky the dog
At the beach
I ran in the sea and Sky followed me.

Amanda Butler (8)
Odstock Primary School

HULLABALOO!

A snake is long
A snake is short
A snake is fat
A snake is slim
A snake is slimy
And slithery
A snake is sharp
And fine
A snake is shapely
And athletic
A snake is called
A boa constrictor
A snake is called
An adder
A snake is called
A python
A snake is called
A rattler
A snake is cold-blooded.

Patrick Henderson (9)
Odstock Primary School

HULLABALOO!

My dog is playful
He jumps so high
He could touch the sky
He looks so brown he shines
I threw a ball
He thundered down the hill.

Tom Reed (8)
Odstock Primary School

HULLABALOO!

It's April the 14th, 1943,
All the guns are firing,
And the planes are going *whee*,
Whilst they're fighting.

German planes are coming,
All this signals for
Apprehension,
They are coming.

The great battle has come,
The battle for Britain,
This is not that fun,
The German planes are here.

German planes are coming,
Coming for our lives,
It's invasion yes,
They are coming.

The soldiers running forward,
Followed by the tanks,
Germans are forced backwards,
It is VE day!

The German planes are fleeing,
Fleeing for their lives,
It's retreat yes,
They are leaving.

All the church bells ringing,
The people shouting loud,
Thank you to the army,
For saving that big crowd.

Andrew Labdon (10)
Odstock Primary School

HULLABALOO!

Rickety, rockety, chugging along,
People waving, bells making a bong,
Suddenly rocketing down a hill,
People screaming, checking the bill,
Whizz round the corner,
Lurch to a stop.

Slowly, slowly, round and round,
Parents have to pay a pound.
Faster, faster have a go,
Slows back down, slow, slow, slow,
Gently whirring
To a halt.

Horn blaring, car starting,
Ticket man shouting, people darting,
Oops, there's a car racing towards us,
Swivel round and drive at the speed of a bus,
Ram the car, a car rams me,
Horn blares again,
Time to stop.

Wow, look at the time,
Let's get home, it's nearly nine!
I've had a great time.

Sarah-Jane Harris (9)
Odstock Primary School

THE COLD COUNTRYSIDE

It's a cold day in the countryside
The countryside is far and wide
The herds of sheep and hanging cows
Standing there
Not moving a hair.

The sky is getting dark
As the hovering skylark
Hovers around our house
As quiet as a mouse
The wind blows through the trees
Ascends down the tumbling leaves.

Holly Risdon (9)
Roundstone Preparatory School

THE SKY AT NIGHT

On a cold winter's time
I look at the sky at night
The sky looks so dark
But the moon looks so bright.

I look at the window
Sitting on my chair
And I say to myself,
I wonder how many stars are out there?

My dad says there are millions
Of stars out in space
It makes Earth seem
Such a small place

I look at the stars
With a feeling of hope
And I bring them closer
With my telescope.

They say they are all suns
Just like ours
Is there a boy like me?
Looking at ours.

Lewis Davis (9)
Roundstone Preparatory School

THE COUNTRYSIDE IN SUMMER

I love the countryside
The trees stand tall and small
The grass is lush and green
Tracks where people have been.

The wild flowers gently sway
The horses feed off the hay
The bees eat the pollen with ease
In the gentle summer breeze.

The cows wander around fields
As farmers look to their yields
The sheep are seen to gather together
Hoping always to stay forever.

The countryside
Is far and wide
At least look after it
With pride.

Olivia Evans (11)
Roundstone Preparatory School

OUR WORLD

Our world has lots of different weather,
Like sun, rain and snow.
A lot of this weather is always together,
And the temperature can be very low.

Our world has lots of different animals,
Like whales, dogs and cats.
A lot of these animals can be mammals,
Such as humans, who are the best at that.

Our world has lots of different food,
Like vegetables, fruit and meat.
A lot of this food can change our mood,
And is very good to eat.

Our world has lots of beautiful things,
Wondrous in its own way.
Such as a bird which has golden wings,
Or the sun setting over the bay.

Eleanor Woods (11)
Roundstone Preparatory School

WINTER'S DAY

On the 21st of December
The first winter's day.
Nothing like November
Because reindeer pull the sleigh.

Rudolph with his nose so bright
The house is full of joy.
Saint Nicholas is coming tonight
Bringing at least one toy.

The day of lots of surprises
Is coming to a start.
Outside are lots of magpies
Writing my new year's chart.

Snowdrops are coming up soon
The start of super spring.
Late rise of the early moon
When bluebirds start to sing.

Samuel Trapp (9)
Roundstone Preparatory School

My Hobbies

My favourite hobby is football
I play it every week.
My boots are made from leather
And I hope they don't leak.
I also swim for Trowbridge
I train three times a week.
My hat's made of silicone
And I wear flippers on my feet.
I have a bike for my birthday
The tyres are big and chunky.
When I ride down the park
The roads seem very bumpy.
I like to play sport every day
It makes me fit and healthy.
I hope I can one day
Play sport and be wealthy.

John Carroll (9)
Roundstone Preparatory School

Sun

Sun is yellow, sun is hot
It sits up in that sky most of the day
It makes me smile when I'm down
Sun is the best all the year round
Sun is yellow, sun is hot
I love sun it's got the looks
It's the best in all the weeks
And June, July and August too
And most of the year round.

Grace Warden (10)
Roundstone Preparatory School

MY IMAGINATION

My imagination
Is an inspiration
My friends think me a fool
To talk about a ghost or a ghoul
Maybe a witch or a wizard
Or sometimes a sandstorm blizzard.

My imagination
Is a sensation
My friends are forced into hysteria
When I talk about a dinosaur in the wisteria!
And then there was a story about a mouse
Who found himself trapped in his own little house.

Katie Allen (9)
Roundstone Preparatory School

LOTTIE'S POEM

I have a dog, she's black and gold,
She likes to run and play,
She also barks and is very bold,
In her very own special way.

Her pet name is Lottie
She's so daft she has me in fits,
Her real nickname is Potty
And I love her to bits.

There isn't any more to say
Except to give this dog its day.

Connor McLaren (9)
Roundstone Preparatory School

WAITING FOR SPRING

One day I looked out of the window,
Hoping spring had arrived,
But no it had not.
There were no flower buds
Or birds singing.
Not even a snowdrop to be seen,
Just frost!
The next day I looked out of the window,
And what a surprise
Spring had arrived!
The flower buds were out,
The birds were singing,
Even the snowdrops were here,
And no frost!

Abigail Little (9)
Roundstone Preparatory School

SEARCHING FOR A WHALE

A whale is a wonderful creature
And has the most amazing features.
It lives deep under the sea,
As dark as dark can be.
It has a blowhole on its head,
Which reaches to the seabed.
On its back there's a dorsal fin,
Which can be either thick or thin.
A whale can be lots of colours, blue, black or grey
And you'll find them swimming there,
On that one perfect day.

Miriam Stevens (9)
Roundstone Preparatory School

SEASIDE

My family and I are going to the beach
To run in the sand and jump in the sea
To get wet in the water and covered in sand
And splash and jump until our heart is content

We will eat and drink all we like
Our picnic is filled with lots of delights
We will fill ourselves up and drink lots of pop
And we will lie in the sun until the day is done

The day is over the beach has gone
The people are leaving and the tide is in
The umbrellas are down the seagulls are gone
As we climb into our cars as the day is done.

Lucy Bush (10)
Roundstone Preparatory School

AUTUMN

The leaves are falling from the trees
Autumn is here, autumn is here.
The leaves are turning from green to red,
Autumn is here, autumn is here.
The trees are colourful, orange, red and brown,
Autumn is here, autumn is here.
The birds fly south, in the shape of a V,
Autumn is here, autumn is here.
The moon comes sooner, the sun is late,
Autumn is here, autumn is here.
Wait a minute there's frost and snow covered trees,
Winter is here, and autumn is gone.

Victoria Farrell (9)
Roundstone Preparatory School

FRIENDS

Every lady should have a friend,
A friend is something special,
It doesn't matter if they're small
Or even if they are tall.

A good friend is someone you trust,
Who doesn't go and tell all your secrets,
It doesn't matter how old they are
As long as they're good and loyal.

A friend is someone who wants to play,
A friend that wants to stay all day,
A friend is always kind and helpful,
And will be your friend forever.

Alice Carroll (10)
Roundstone Preparatory School

SNOW

Winter is the time for snow to fall,
Laying a thick, white blanket over the land.
Oh snow, snow lying on the ground,
Sparkling and glistening.
Oh cover everything in your winter wonderland.
When snow falls everything looks magical.
You can make snow angels, snowmen,
Anything.
So go on! Play in the *snow*!

Amber Kennedy (9)
Roundstone Preparatory School

THE SNOWMAN

As I looked out of the windows to see
If my snowman was there.
There he stood in the bright cold air.
I picked up my hat and coat and
Slowly walked outside.

The fresh air was blowy as I
Looked all around.
The clouds in the sky and snow
On the ground.

I picked up a carrot and put it
In his face.
I took out some buttons from
My brown leather case.

Now he needed a hat or a scarf
And when I put it on him
it just made me laugh.
When he was finished and complete
I wanted to keep him out here,
Away from the heat.

I wished I could keep him
Forever and ever.
But I knew he would come back
Because he was clever.

Charlotte Barrow (9)
Roundstone Preparatory School

BEYOND THE WATERS

The sea is a building, carved with elegance,
With treasured secrets ready to be found,
Distant footsteps search for hidden pages of history,
Smashed ink pots stain the forbidden papers,
Scheming ladders make a draught,
As they fly past the librarian's desk,
Ancient pages weep in the darkness.
Creatures hold their breath, afraid to break,
The blood-sucking silence,
And the library sign
Swings,
Swings,
Swings . . .

Eleanor Ridge (11)
St Andrew's CE Primary School, Swindon

THE SEA

The sea is flat roofed, with smooth blue
Slates shimmering in the moonlight.
Its ornate door is mould covered,
Oozing moss clings to seven foot tall shelves.
Books that are mysterious and magical,
Hide their rusty locks guarding mischief,
Moaning sounds emerge from wordless pages.
Souls of sadness, from people who have been
Stuck there forever, drift into the darkness.

Holly Goldsmith (11)
St Andrew's CE Primary School, Swindon

THE SEA

The sea is a building carved out with elegance,
With hidden secrets waiting to be found,
Distant footsteps search for pages of history,
Smashed ink pots stain the forbidden pages.
Sliding ladders make a chilling breeze
Ancient pages weep in the darkness.
Spiders hold their breath
Afraid to break the everlasting silence.
Dust tornadoes spin, choking the clear, cold air.
But the oak wooden door swings on it hinges
Swings,
Swings,
Swings . . .

Emily Harrison (10)
St Andrew's CE Primary School, Swindon

THE SEA

The sea is an ancient, dust-filled museum,
Its wooden doors open a mystery,
All is still,
Silent
Until . . .
Strangled screams echo from a mummified tomb,
The cracked marble floor reflects shadows.
Cordoned off areas hidden from view
Still statues with staring eyes
Whispers fade in the darkness . . .

Sophie Lloyd (11)
St Andrew's CE Primary School, Swindon

STUTTERING STROLL DOWN THE TOWN

The rain falls in the town,
The houses stare at me,
As I stroll by.
The school screams,
'Come and learn now,'
As I zoom past in my car,
The trees grab out at me,
With their sharp claws.
The shops scream out, 'We want customers,'
The drainpipe talks,
'I need water.'
The dustbins vomit out rubbish at me
As I stroll by.

Jack Thompson (11)
St Andrew's CE Primary School, Swindon

THE SEA

The sea is hidden beneath the surface
People are crowded and cramped.
You can hear the echoing of cries
Screams of lost souls sobbing,
Slamming shut bars.
Echo from deep underground
Chains chatter and clatter from all around.
Footsteps click from every direction.
Guards patrol the perimeter
Watching for escapees.

Georgie Castle (11)
St Andrew's CE Primary School, Swindon

THE SEA

The sea is a modern building
Hidden behind shiny glass doors.
Its questioning screams
Bounce from wall to wall,
Ringing around the room.
The sea's marble floor
Shines in the sun,
As it reflects its smoothness,
Through the open doors.
Glaring behind glass cages
It's seen but not to be heard.
The cries of the extinct animals
Screaming, 'Let us out!'
Echoing around the empty halls,
Left all alone.

Chris Walker (10)
St Andrew's CE Primary School, Swindon

THE SEA

The sea opens its arms to me,
With ancient doors black and long.
Ancient books few smudged pages,
To be seen by the human eye.
Skeletons click and move,
Swinging to and fro.
Echoes and footprints go through
To an ancient land.

Angellina Marie Nagitta (10)
St Andrew's CE Primary School, Swindon

MY DRIVE

The dustbin gobbled rubbish as I drove by.
The drain choked as some of the rubbish tried to get in.
Trees tried to grab the car as I sped by.
The river was drowning
As I climbed over the bridge's arched back.
Shops shouted out, 'Come and spend in the sale.'
Lamp posts shone like a spotlight,
Their eyes following the car.

Hannah Carter (11)
St Andrew's CE Primary School, Swindon

SECRETS OF THE SEA

The sea washes up the skeletons that lie slouching
In the towers dead or alive?
Blood trickles down step by step, down, down, down
Into the hall.
The sea tortures itself with its own horrific memories
And then an eerie silence descends
And places a cape of darkness,
As ancient bodies hang in the manacle.

Matthew Sweeney (11)
St Andrew's CE Primary School, Swindon

MY JOURNEY

I walked up the stairs
My growling bed beckoned me.
I thought to myself,
Will I ever go on my journey again?

Stephanie Moore (11)
St Andrew's CE Primary School, Swindon

IMAGINE

Dragon cars fly by,
As smoke flows out of the radiator.

Lamp posts light the way,
When they open their eyes.

Trees crash on the ground,
Stopping cars from striding past their shadows.

Houses greet you with their friendly welcome,
'Come in and have a cup of tea.'

Dustbins gobble garbled speech,
As you interrupt them with your litter.

Shops persuade you with their persuasive words,
'Come in and spend your money.'

Adam Beasant
St Andrew's CE Primary School, Swindon

THE SEA

The sea has a wooden door that opens a deep dark
Secret,
All is quiet,
Until . . . the strangled scream echoes from a mummified
Mummy.
The sea's dark marble floor reflects a sodden mystery,
Roped off areas, hidden from far off view.
Still statues with eyes of mystery,
Whispers fade in the darkness

Hannah Glass (10)
St Andrew's CE Primary School, Swindon

THE SEA

The sea has ten foot tall bookcases,
Keeping you locked inside forever.
Books lying torn there, without any words.
One flickering candle burns down to the end of its wax.
A trail of forbidden, silky cobwebs
Lead to a man, a dead man,
Lying there with a dagger through his throat.
As spiders feed off his ripped, squidgy eyeballs.
In the corner the old owner sits there in his armchair,
With an evil grin on his face,
Waiting . . . waiting . . . for another man to enter.

James Fairclough & Josh Jones (10)
St Andrew's CE Primary School, Swindon

THE OCEAN

The ocean is a haunted forest
Saturated with 1,000 ghosts,
Spirits hidden in the corner
Draped in silky cobwebs.
Sparks of light gleam out of the sad soul,
Screams echo throughout the everlasting trees,
Gnarled roots scrape their grinding claws,
Dark,
Damp,
Dank bats swoop overhead.

Sophie Bell (11)
St Andrew's CE Primary School, Swindon

MY JOURNEY

The house called me in for tea as I rushed past,
The car rocked me to sleep as I flopped down,
Trees screamed for me to climb them.
The church called me in to pray,
The colleges shouted like my teacher,
Bins spat out rubbish but I just ran home.

Samantha Cowie (10)
St Andrew's CE Primary School, Swindon

MY MUM

I don't know what
I'd do without my
Mum!

She's wonderful,
She's pretty,
She's confident and determined.
She's great,
She's caring,
She's clever,
She's fun,
She's sweet,
She's sunny and bright,
She's always happy,
She's considerate,
She's kind,
She's lovely,
She's sharing
She's interesting
And I love her.

Bryony Mason (11)
St George's School, Warminster

MUM ...!

Mum, can you tie my shoe?
Mum, can you clean the loo?
Mum, can you comb my hair?
Mum, can you wash the stair?
Mum, can you pack my lunch?
Mum, can you feel this punch?
Mum, can you wipe my face?
Mum, can you offer me plaice?
Mum, can you learn to prance?
Mum, can you perform a dance?
Mum, can you sing to me?
Mum, can you prepare my tea?
Mum, can you pass me sherry?
Mum, can you pick a cherry?
Mum, can you control the world?
Mum, can you award me that pearl?
Mum, can you stop the riot?
Mum, can you ...
Son, please be quiet!

Rory Walsh (10)
St George's School, Warminster

MY MUM

My mum, my mum she is the best
My mum, my mum she needs a good rest
My mum, my mum she is so lovely
My mum, my mum she gives me money
My mum, my mum she is so funny
My mum, my mum she is so sunny.

Cristina Fordham (10)
St George's School, Warminster

MY MOTHER

Mummy, Mummy, dear,
When nightmares occur,
You take away my fear.
Frantically rushing
Every day,
You never get time to go away!
Helping around the house
As quiet as a tiny mouse.
Always caring,
Never a time goes by when you're not sharing.
Beautiful, glorious, ray of sunshine,
Whistling like a windchime.
A bumper box of crunchy chocolates,
A glass of smooth red wine or two,
I would like to take this chance to say,
You are the best!
Better than the rest!

Philippa Wall (11)
St George's School, Warminster

MUM

Hey my mum is great,
My mum is fun,
My mum is brighter than the sun.
My mum has a great sense of humour,
She is attracted to the Hoover,
My mum helps me all day.
My mum helps me in all sorts of ways,
She's like a bee she never stops,
She always does the weekly shop.

Adam Holman (11)
St George's School, Warminster

Mum

If I didn't have a mum like you
Wow I would be in a stew.
Who would wash and iron my clothes?
Goodness only knows!

If I didn't have a mum like you
Wow I would be in a stew
No one to cook, or clean, or help
Me tidy up my bookshelf.

If I didn't have a mum like you
Wow I would be in a stew.
Who would cut and prune the trees,
Or clear away all the weeds?

If I didn't have a mum like you
Wow I would be in a stew.
Who would travel to the shops,
For chips, pizza and pork chops?

If I didn't have a mum like you
Wow I would be in a stew.
If you didn't do all these things for me
I'd have no breakfast, lunch or tea.

So just to say thanks ever so much
For breakfast, dinner, tea and lunch;
And for everything else you do for me.
Without you I don't know where I'd be.

And now I'm really glad to say,
I have a mum like you, hooray!

Alexandra Andow (10)
St George's School, Warminster

MUM

My mum is the best mum
The best mum for me
She clothes and feeds me
And always keeps me warm

My mum is the best mum
The best mum for me
She tackles all my washing
And cares for me

My mum is the best mum
The best mum for me
She transports me to school each day
And homework she encourages me

My mum is the best mum
The best mum for me
She drives me to swimming each night
And galas across the country.

My mum is the best mum
The best mum for me
She helps me in my needs
And is rarely cross with me

My mum is the best mum
The best mum for me
She is everything I love
She is the perfect mum for me.

Dominique Aston
St George's School, Warminster

LET'S SPOIL MUM

Today, Mum, it's your special day!
Hip, hip, hip, hooray!
It's time to spoil you completely rotten,
With flowers, chocolates and jumpers of cotton.

Today, Mum, it's your special day!
Hip, hip, hip, hooray!
No chores or back breaking work for you,
Time to do something exciting and new!

Today, Mum, it's your special day!
Hip, hip, hip, hooray!
Forget the laundering of my clothes
Enjoy a dainty, delicate rose!

Today, Mum, it's your special day!
Hip, hip, hip, hooray!
Don't bother to prepare the lunch
I'll do it for you . . . munch, munch, munch!

Happy Mother's Day

Sarah Devoy (11)
St George's School, Warminster

MY MUM

My mum is loving, she always helps me,
My mum is thoughtful, she endlessly cooks my tea,
My mum is caring, she likes me sharing,
My mum is tidy, she finds me wearing,
My mum is hilarious, we have masses of fun,
My mum is constantly there for me, I love you Mum!

Charles Allardice (11)
St George's School, Warminster

MOTHER'S DAY

Tulips are red, delphiniums are blue,
I'm sure Dad doesn't regret marrying you.

Some mums are rather funny,
Some mums are sunny,
Some mums are kind and caring,
Some mums like sharing.

Tulips are red, delphiniums are blue,
I'm sure Dad doesn't regret marrying you.

Some mums are smart,
Some mums have kind, gentle hearts,
Some mums are sporty,
Some mums can be naughty.

Tulips are red, delphiniums are blue,
I'm sure Dad doesn't regret marrying you.

You are my angel without wings.

Cariad Wright (11)
St George's School, Warminster

MY MOTHER

M is my mother who helps me all day
          in every single way.
O is no other mother like you, you cheer me up
          when I am feeling blue.
T is the table you help me to lay.
H is the horrible dreams you keep away.
E is excellent in what you wear.
R is reliable, you are always there.

James Baysting
St George's School, Warminster

MOTHER'S DAY

M is for mum who feeds me.
O is for oven that cooks my tea.
T is for table where my mum puts my dinner.
H is for hockey what my mum hates to do.
E is for extra help that my mum gives to me.
R is for radiant that my mum looks to me.
S is for smiling that my mum always does.

D is for danger that my mum protects me from.
A is for assistance that my mum gives to me.
Y is for yes that my mum always says to me.

Kyle Byrne
St George's School, Warminster

I LOVE MUM

I   ndividual, different from all the others

L   ike all other mothers
O   ffers me sweets all the time
V   ery sensible, never miserable
E   veryone's number one

M   akes me laugh
U   ses bubbles in her bath
M   akes sure I'm tucked in at night, my mum's the best
         I know I'm right.

Hannah Rea (11)
St George's School, Warminster

MUM

Mum so far as my life with you,
Has been full of laughter, fun days too!

You always support me in what I do,
You're lovely and kind at weekends too!

I think you're the best mum ever,
I will love you forever!

You're under pressure all day through,
I've just got one thing to ask:
Really where would I be without you?

Abi Blagdon (10)
St George's School, Warminster

MUM

Here it comes, Mother's Day.
A chance to spoil Mum, hooray!
Here comes the question, now I worry.
I must buy Mum a present, and hurry.
What would my wonderful Mum need?
Creamy chocolates, colourful flowers, a book to read?
There must be something she has in mind.
That is what I must find.
I've had my thought, now my idea.
How about a poem, Mother dear?

Ellen Tansey (10)
St George's School, Warminster

My Mum Is Magic

My mum is magic in every way
The washing's there and gone the next day.
My mum is clever, loving too
She taught me how to tie my shoes.

My mum is magic in every way
The washing's there and gone the next day.
She's gentle, generous, never rude
She always makes me superb food.

My mum is magic in every way
The washing's there and gone the next day.
She's helpful, obliging, never mean
She always keeps the house so clean.

My mum is magic in every way
The washing's there and gone the next day.

I love you Mum!

Yasmin Galbraith (11)
St George's School, Warminster

Mum

My mum is very special,
She's oh so kind to me.
The reasons are so obvious
And very plain to see.

She really loves me very much,
She's lovely, warm and caring
And when she says she loves me,
She shows it's true by sharing.

Whenever I need help from her
I know that it will come
And I can always count on her,
My very special . . . Mum!

Emma Hutchinson (10)
St George's School, Warminster

MUM

My mum, my mum.

My mum is the best
She is better than the rest
She helps me every day
In every sort of way.

My mum, my mum.

My mum is great
She is never late
I see her every day
She never goes away.

My mum, my mum.

My mum she feeds me so well
She helps me if I fail
She is really fun
And brighter than the sun

My mum, my mum.

I do love you
And I hope you do too.

Ashley Holman (11)
St George's School, Warminster

I NEED A FRIEND

I turn up at school
And they call me a fool,
They take the Mick because I wear glasses,
Matt, kicking a ball at me as he passes.
I don't care
When they make fun of my hair!
When they throw me in dirt
And ruin my shirt.

But all I want is a friend,
Someone who I can play with,
Who I can trust,
Who I can talk to,
Who I can tell secrets to,
Life is boring without a friend
Someone help me!
I need a friend.

Joseph Burrows (11)
St John's RC School, Trowbridge

SPRING IS HERE

The adder slithers, hungry for food,
The winter over, he's in predator mood.
New growth everywhere in the wood,
Spring's returned this time hopefully for good.
Quickly following a mouse's scent
The adder pauses to see where it went.
Timing it right, quick as a flash!
Spring sun blazing, mouse is mash.

Jack Rosier (10)
St John's RC School, Trowbridge

SPOOKSTER

Spookster DJs and skateboards,
This is done under the floorboards,
He's a ghost of course,
It's quite clear
That a DJ ghost is very queer,
Normal people get on with their lives,
But down below Spookster jives and jives.

All his ghoully friends are cool,
They all pop down to the spooky mall,
Spookster says DJs are cool,
But then again that's Spookster's rule!
His dead long dream is to MC,
To hold rock parties for you and me,
But he DJs to fill him with glee!

Peter Hammond (9)
St John's RC School, Trowbridge

SPRING

A snowdrop popped out! It's spring!
What a lovely thing to sing.
Spring is here, let's all cheer.
Let's make the most of it while it's here.
Watch the birds and lambs being born.
Watch the beautiful sky in the morn.
Winter has gone, everything is growing.
Buds are appearing, the colours are glowing.
The world is alive, with life once more.
This is the season I adore.

Sarah Devereux (10)
St John's RC School, Trowbridge

THE SPRING FARM

It was springtime on the farm
And everything seemed pretty calm,
Tanya tabby cat had four kittens,
Each very cute with black and white mittens.

Carly cow stood proudly tall,
While her calf was wobbling very small,
Daisy the sheepdog was watching near,
While her pups raced in their highest gear.

Harriet hen had 6 chicks,
But poor Danny donkey was just practising his kicks,
'What's wrong?' asked his fellow mate,
'Everyone's got a baby, I want a date!'

So Pauline pig, Danny's best mate,
Put posters around the farm to try and get a date,
They sat by the phone all day long,
But had no luck so they sang a sad song.

They went to sleep and woke up early,
For the phone rang, it was the pretty donkey Shirley,
'Hi,' she said, 'You must be Danny,
I'll come and see you for you live by my Nanny.'

The very next month, Shirley and Danny were married,
At the end of it all, they were both drunk and had to be carried,
The following spring Shirley had twins,
Now Danny was happy and not down in the bins!

Stephanie McGee (11)
St John's RC School, Trowbridge

VAMPIRE DRACK

There once was a vampire called Vampire Drack
He ate half New York and his feelings were black
Police on his tail he will never look back
The name of course was Vampire Drack.

His lair was secret and underground
Vampire Drack and a killer hound
Perfect combination you might think
For chasing mice under kitchen sinks.

Vampire Drack and the killer hound
Were chasing people round and round
In your house and on the street
They might have you as a treat.

Nick Rodgerson (10)
St John's RC School, Trowbridge

FRIENDSHIP

Friendship is like a star at night
Which appears and disappears
The one that stays is the one that glows.

Friendship is like a flower in the summer
A flower that softly sways in the wind
The sun shining to make it grow.

In friendship people come to make friends with you
And play with you all day long
They share stuff with you
They tell you their secrets.

Friendship is my life.

Gemma Giles (10)
St John's RC School, Trowbridge

SPRING

It's a new year
The birds sing
Spring is here.

All the snow melts off the ground
Flowers show
Blooms come up
Spring is here.

The sun shines
It wakes up from its sleep
Spring is here
Spring, spring, spring
Flowers, flowers, flowers
They're waiting on the garden step.

Sean Patrick Bridle (10)
St John's RC School, Trowbridge

SPRING

Spring is here, winter is over.
Fields are full of bright green clover.
Buds are growing on the trees.
Full of beautiful cherry leaves.

Newborn lambs are being born.
Farmers are planting seeds for corn.
Daffodil bulbs are being planted.
Everyone's spring wish is being granted.

Lauren Binder (9)
St John's RC School, Trowbridge

DOGS

Some dogs are spotty.
Some dogs are brown.
But my dog is surely,
The best dog in town.

Some dogs are big.
Some dogs are small.
But my dog is in the middle,
The best dog in town.

Some dogs are beautiful,
Some dogs wear ribbons.
But my dog has a trophy,
The best dog in town.

Emma Bracey (9)
St John's RC School, Trowbridge

SPRING

Spring is here
Winter is over
The fields are filled with four-leafed clover
Buds are growing on the trees
Full of beautiful cherry leaves
What a long wait, at last spring is here.

In the fields the sheep are breeding
New baby lambs are on the way
The mother soon will be feeding
Her lamb in every way.

Faye Vanstone (10)
St John's RC School, Trowbridge

SPRING

Spring is here,
Blossom is seen.
Singing is heard,
From beautiful birds
And all is well.
The sun is out,
Children play about.
The sky is blue,
The sea is too,
All is well.
Kids kick stones,
Parents eat scones,
People sunbathe on the beach,
While other people suck a peach.
All is well it's spring!

Charlotte Waller (11)
St John's RC School, Trowbridge

ASSEMBLY

A   ll in the hall silent as a mouse,
S   itting on the floor suffering pins and needles,
S   itting with our back straight, arms folded,
E   ach person suffering of boredom,
M   anic to get out, people falling over, 'Oh dear,'
B   lasting out into the playground,
L   eaving the hall was the best thing today,
Y   es, yes free, *wow*.

Hannah Anderson (10)
St John's RC School, Trowbridge

THE FUNFAIR

Up, up and away soaring day and night,
Throw the loop down and down.
Nervously we go up and turn around
Down! Down we go zooming past everyone,
Bumpety, bump the journey's just been done.

Round and round, up and down, seeing everyone!
Peering on my horse racing everyone, wondering
When I'll stop.

Round and round right up high!
Peering down, far far down
Peering down, up up high
And coming to a
Stop!

Thomas Miller (9)
St John's RC School, Trowbridge

SPORT

Rugby, rugby
Try to get muddy!
Tennis, tennis
You have to hit the ball!
Football, football
You have to kick the ball!
Badminton, badminton
You have to hit the shuttlecock!
Sport, sport
It's so fun!

Simon Stafford (10)
St John's RC School, Trowbridge

FRIENDS

F is for friends. They're there through thick and thin.
R is for relationship. Fragile as a glass cup.
I is for impossible. For us not to be friends.
E is for everlasting. That is our friendship.
N is for never-ending. That is the road of friendship.
D is for dagger. It could pierce your friendship.
S is for sunny. Sunny times with your friends.
H is for honoured. That I am!
I is for isolation. That is where you are when your friends go away.
P is for perfect. That is my friendship!

Sarah Jones (10)
St John's RC School, Trowbridge

SPRING

It's the 21st March
And a lot of people are sitting under an arch.
The rabbits are waking up from their nice long rest
And the birds are in their warm and cosy nests.
So what about me?
I'm in my bed
Cuddled up with my great big ted.

Christopher Raymond (11)
St John's RC School, Trowbridge

ST PAUL'S

St Paul's School is where I go.
To learn all the things I should know.
English, maths and history too.
And lots of fun things for me to do.

Stacey Vincent (8)
Sarum St Paul's Primary School, Salisbury

THE SEASONS

Bright sunny daffodils sprouting from the ground.
Children running in the park and playing with their balls.
Pink and white blossoms growing on fruit trees.
Spring.

Leafy trees rustling in the summer breeze.
People of all sorts licking cold ice lollies.
Children running and screaming on the hot sandy beach.
Summer.

Crispy brown leaves falling from twiggy trees.
People in new, shiny wellies splashing in big, muddy puddles.
Dogs barking madly in neat, tidy parks.
Autumn.

White blanket covering the ground.
Icy snowflakes falling from the cloudy grey sky.
Footprints in every direction.
Winter.

Catherine Simpson (9)
Sarum St Paul's Primary School, Salisbury

THE ELEPHANT

A giant grey ship of the African plains
Watching the smaller animals go by,
As it travels across the baking ground it has no worry for lions,
This armoured tank can't be stopped by any fellow creatures,
Only man will bring him down,
The elephant started a journey he would not finish,
Soon he will part this mortal plain never to return.

Jacob Stanistreet (10)
Sarum St Paul's Primary School, Salisbury

THE WINTER

Winter's breath biting cold
Blowing trees big and old
Moving past till leaves depart
Blowing over truck and cart.

Eyes making sparks from above
Making all run in its path;
Voice bellowing, voice moaning
Voice whispering, voice groaning.

Lots of leaves on the floor
Crusted old live no more
Winter kicking with a shout
Making them fly about.

James Neville (10)
Sarum St Paul's Primary School, Salisbury

BLACK

In the midst of the woods,
Smoke of death will appear,
The centre of Hell so mysterious,
Covered in spirits of hatred.

The death of war remains still evil,
As the mysterious clock strikes midnight,
The dead appear in mystical smoke,
As the evil ones disintegrate,
In the powerful gush of light.

Rebecca Baker (10)
Sarum St Paul's Primary School, Salisbury

PURPLE

The shivering night
Feeling the cold
Which the wind brings with it
As it lingers around.

Flowers falling from the branches
Leaving the trees bare
Until the next spring
When blossoms grow.

A flock of birds
A pattern in the cool breeze
One winter's night.

Jennifer Dawson (10)
Sarum St Paul's Primary School, Salisbury

ROSES

As pretty as a princess
As pink as a baby
With light drops of water caressing the petals.

The silken petals soft and smooth
Shimmering like a ruby
But staying still like a diamond
The leaves sway gently in the breeze.

And everything is silent.

Poppy Short (11)
Sarum St Paul's Primary School, Salisbury

I SHOULD LIKE TO ...

I should like to paint the quietness of an empty classroom,
Before the children creep in.

To hear the sound of a summer's breeze through the tiger's fur,
As they catch their prey.

I should like to see the sea creatures sleeping
As they settle between the reefs.

I should like to capture the water
As it trickless down the fall.

I should like to feel the sensation of the sunset,
As it sinks into another life.

I should like to paint the crackle of a fire,
As it gets lit on a winter's night!

Lorraine Dawson (11)
Sarum St Paul's Primary School, Salisbury

I WOULD LIKE ...

I would like to hear the moonlight glowing.
I would like to feel the wind.

I would like to see the air.
I would like to smell the wood.

I would like to taste the lantern of the light.
I would like to hear space.

I would like to touch the coldness of the air.
I would like to see the wind rushing.

Jack Stead (10)
Sarum St Paul's Primary School, Salisbury

BLACK

The town is silent as evil creeps in
It lurks into houses, the sky and within.

The candles shiver as it draws near midnight.

It's too late now the evil is in fast flight.
Amongst the trees they whisper frightened in despair.

Swaying in the mist, is the evil there?
Death is now arising the Hell mouth is now here.

Everyone is running, everyone should fear
The eyes are looking out. What shall the people do?
The eyes are looking out, watching over you!

Stephanie Hatchman (11)
Sarum St Paul's Primary School, Salisbury

MY BAD DREAM

I had a bad dream,
So I woke up and started to scream.

My mummy came in and calmed me down,
I said to her I had a bad dream of a scary clown.

Next thing I knew it was morning
My dad was still asleep and I heard him snoring.

'I hate school,' he said, yawning
'Oh it's really boring.'

I had a great time at school
Because everyone thinks that I'm really cool.

Melissa Crouch (8)
Sarum St Paul's Primary School, Salisbury

I WOULD LIKE . . .

I would like to taste the centre of the earth.
I would like to feel what it's like to be a mountain.
I would like to smell an eagle's egg.
I would like to see the end of a rainbow.
I would like to hear Africa cry for rain.
I would like to separate the sea in two.
I would like to sense danger coming.

Michael Shaw (10)
Sarum St Paul's Primary School, Salisbury

I WOULD LIKE TO . . .

I would like to see a painting in action.
I would like to smell the flames of the sun up close.
I would like to feel a shark's tooth when it's alive.
I would like to hear a book talk.
I would like to taste electricity flowing.

Alicia Murphy
Sarum St Paul's Primary School, Salisbury

I WOULD LIKE . . .

I would like to taste a cheesy moon.
I would like to see my voice floating around.
I would like to touch a rainbow.
I would like to smell the flames of the sun.
I would like to hear money.

Lauren Crockett (10)
Sarum St Paul's Primary School, Salisbury

I WOULD LIKE . . .

I would like to hear a flower scream.
I would like to see my voice.
I would like to touch a comet's tail.
I would like to taste the heat of the sun.
I would like to smell the sound of music.
I would like to understand the language of a cat.

Louis Bennett (10)
Sarum St Paul's Primary School, Salisbury

THOUGHTS

I would like to feel the heat of an asteroid.
I would like to paint the feeling of a broken heart.
I would like to smell the rainbow.
I would like to understand the calling of an owl.
I would like to feel the heaviness of a whale.

Conor Sheehan (10)
Sarum St Paul's Primary School, Salisbury

I WOULD LIKE . . .

I would like to paint the screech of a bat.
I would like to taste the tip of a bushfire's flame.
I would like to smell the shine of a star.
I would like to see the speed of light.
I would like to hear a snowflake's heart.

Scott Biddle (10)
Sarum St Paul's Primary School, Salisbury

THE RAINBOW

As I look up and see the rainbow,
Its multicolours are such a glow!
Red, yellow and indigo and green;
All those colours made me keen!
Violet, orange and blue,
Any more, or do you need a clue?
Beautiful colours set in the sky,
I wish I could touch them, I wish I could fly.

All those colours made by sun and rain,
Like the colours you can find in Spain!
The rainbow is arched like a great bridge,
Like the shape of a croissant in the fridge!
But then the rainbow disappears,
The sun stops shining and the rain slowly clears.

Then it turns to cold and damp;
It gets to the evening, when you put on a lamp.
The next day comes, it's the rainbow again!
When the sun shines brightly and down comes the rain.

Lauren Anthony (10)
Sarum St Paul's Primary School, Salisbury

I SHOULD LIKE TO . . .

I should like to see the pieces when dawn breaks,
I should like to paint the sound of a racing car roaring
round a track,
I should like to paint the feelings of a tortoise struggling
up a hill.

Bobby Truckle
Sarum St Paul's Primary School, Salisbury

WINTER

At wintertime,
Cold bites your fingers,
Robins come out to be winter singers.
Sheets of white cover the grass,
As children watch from their class.

Animals are rushingly storing,
While wind whistles loud in the morning.
Leaves are being hastily raked,
As fresh mince pies are being baked.

Trees stand shivering in the cold,
As Christmas tales are being told.
Nice warm fires are being lit,
While everyone gets on a warming kit.

Stacey Winter (10)
Sarum St Paul's Primary School, Salisbury

I SHOULD LIKE TO . . .

I should like to paint the howling wind
Before it roars through the town.

I should like to paint the sound of a crying stone
After being washed out to sea.

I should like to feel a colourful rainbow in the sky
Before it's swept away by the powerful wind.

I should like to paint the feelings of a leaf
As it falls off its sycamore tree.

Hannah Penny (10)
Sarum St Paul's Primary School, Salisbury

ANIMALS

Dogs are smelly
Cats are funny
Hamsters are clean, you know what I mean
Rabbits are fluffy
Guinea pigs are nosy
Parrots are noisy
Pigs are oinky
Worms are squiggly
Hedgehogs are spiky
Fish are shiny
Frogs go *ribbit*
Owls sit on a pole
Bears are scary.

Kirsty Harrison (9)
Sarum St Paul's Primary School, Salisbury

MAGIC

Magic comes and magic goes.
Magic fingers, magic toes.
Magic hands and magic feet.
Magic in my teacher's street.
Magic here and magic there.
Magic pops up everywhere.
Magic moon and magic sun.
Magic is a lot of fun.
Magic day, magic night.
Magic gives an awful fright.

Magic, who needs it?

Denis Twomey (10)
Sarum St Paul's Primary School, Salisbury

BEDTIME

At seven, when I go to bed,
I get such pictures in my head.

Trains and cars,
Jupiter and Mars.

I get these pictures in my head,
At seven, when I go to bed.

Abbie Humphreys (9)
Sarum St Paul's Primary School, Salisbury

PURPLE

The shivering night feeling the cold
Which the wind brings with it
As it lingers around.

Flowers falling from the branches
Leaving the trees bare
Until the next springtime

Louise Helen Dredge (11)
Sarum St Paul's Primary School, Salisbury

BLACK

The sudden gunshot
As a man is killed during war.
A piercing scream
As a child is being tortured.
Clouds covering the earth
As war approaches.

Laura Allen (10)
Sarum St Paul's Primary School, Salisbury

BLUE

As I touch the cold, cold snow,
My heart fills with joy and glow!
Cool, cool seas and warm, warm skies,
All the brown feathered eagles fly!
Under the seas, sand so smooth,
Not one animal dares to move!
Candyfloss clouds far from the ground,
Moving gracefully without a sound!

Zoe Roberts (11)
Sarum St Paul's Primary School, Salisbury

WHEN OUT SHOOTING

When out shooting birds just for fun
Here is something to reflect upon
Would you find it pleasant
To meet a large pheasant
And he was the one with the gun?

Georgina Biffen (8)
Sarum St Paul's Primary School, Salisbury

RED

Blood is creeping in your body.
Death is coming to your school.
I am coming for revenge.
A devil has got your mum
Your eye has got bloodshot.

Ashley Raddy (10)
Sarum St Paul's Primary School, Salisbury

BEDROOM DISASTER

My bedroom is my palace,
But mum says, 'It's a dump.'
I try to keep it tidy,
Or else she gets the hump!

My bedroom is my own space,
It's my own little retreat,
But when I want to sit down,
I've got a job to find a seat!

My bedroom is a messy place,
I love chaos and clutter,
But when mum opens the door,
I usually hear her mutter!

I sometimes find a piece of toast,
Or a mouldy lump of cheese,
When I search high and low
And get down on my knees.

Mum says I'll get pocket money,
If I tidy my room,
I don't know when that will be,
She's hoping it will be soon!

Kristie Scott (10)
Sarum St Paul's Primary School, Salisbury

I SHOULD LIKE TO . . .

Taste the air on a warm summer evening.
Paint the noise of a busy street on a bright summer's day.
Touch the noise of an elephant's roar.

Lucy Paffett (10)
Sarum St Paul's Primary School, Salisbury

MY DAD

My dad is called John
And he weighs a ton,
He's always moaning about who does the chores,
And it's mostly my Mum who cleans the floors.
In his spare time he is always fishing,
But when he comes home there's lots of kissing.
He's losing his hair and biting his nails,
But when it's a quiz he never fails.
One thing's for sure,
We are not very poor,
So my dad is just a crazy old man!

Emma Mundy (10)
Sarum St Paul's Primary School, Salisbury

I SHOULD LIKE TO . . .

I should like to paint the feelings of a cyclone
Tearing round the Pacific.

I should like to hear the powerful rays of the sun
As it glares with wide eyes.

I should like to see the sound of a busy, bustling city
In the heat of an independent country.

I should like to see the sound of the howling wind
As it travels airborne, to its unknown destination.

Charlie Smith (10)
Sarum St Paul's Primary School, Salisbury

OSTRICH BEGAN

For its height
It took the length of a swan's slender neck
Combined with the height of a giraffe's skinny, scrawny legs
And it stood.

For its speed
It took the rapid movement from the sleek cheetah
It took the quickness of the hopping kangaroo
And it ran.

For its colour
It took the blackness of sodden ink
It took the whiteness of clammy snow
And its colour was made.

For its cowardliness
It took the colour yellow and made its golden beak
And hid his head in the sand.

Ostrich was made.

Lauren Neal (11)
Sherston CE Primary School

THE FLAME

Flame is coming, glowing and sharp
Smoky and hot
Spitting and mad

Flame is rising by sizzling and flaring
Luminous and crackling
Blistering and burning

Rachel Edmundson (9)
Sherston CE Primary School

THE CROCODILE

For his teeth

He grasped the sharpness of a sword,
He grasped the whiteness of a strip of paper,
He grasped the longness of a long piece of string.

For his long tail
He stole the strength from an elephant's trunk,
He stole the scales from a fish,
He stole the length from a giraffe's neck.

For his eyes
He seized the evil from a devil,
He seized the coldness from a lump of ice,
He seized colour from a rainbow.

For his strength
He snatched the muscles from a hippo,
He snatched the agility from a cheetah.

For his long snout
He captured the length from a spade,
He captured the fatness from an elephant.

And crocodile, sneaky as he can get, was made.

Euan Littlejohns (10)
Sherston CE Primary School

FIRE POEM

Fire is the enemy, just waiting to strike.
Flaming and billowing, a blaze of light.
Creeping and swirling across the lands.
Screaming and roaring, criminal in its hands.

A raging temper, spitting and feared.
There's nothing in the world more frightening and weird.
A bubbling anger feared for always.
Sweeps life away in one quick blaze.

Amalie Smith (10)
Sherston CE Primary School

THE CROCODILE

Crocodile began . . .

For his face
He stole two, sharp, jagged orange gems for his eyes,
He snatched a thousand sparkling daggers for his teeth,
And he seized the sly grin of *death*.

For his strength,
He grabbed the force of an army,
He stole the muscles of a strong man,
And he captured the quickness and the sharpness of a sword.

For his long tail,
He seized the power of a world ruler,
He grasped the length of a tree trunk,
And the lash of a mighty whip!

For his rough skin and scales,
He imprisoned the rock mountainside,
The bark of a tree,
And the rough gravel of stony ground.

And Crocodile - King of Waters,
Was made.

Harry Smith (10)
Sherston CE Primary School

GIRAFFE

Jigsaw puzzle
In an abstract shape,
Dappled shadows of the desert,
Earthy colours and exotic patterns.

Church tower
Looming above all beasts,
Gracefully sweeping through the skies,
Reaching, bending, stretching.

Frayed sailor's rope
Gently swaying in the breeze,
Thin and wiry, but soft.

Rubber band
Long, grey and slobbery,
Stretches out to scoop up food.

Flagpoles
Rising above the dusty earth,
Supporting an arrogant but beautiful creature.

It was Giraffe.

Victoria Price (11)
Sherston CE Primary School

FIRE ACROSTIC

F   ire is a missile in a heart.
I   ce is fire's enemy.
R   aging fire will kill you!
E   veryone is being watched.

Sam Armstrong (10)
Sherston CE Primary School

LEOPARD

Leopard began in the summer sunshine.

The golden of the yellow grass
And the jigsaw puzzle pattern
He took for his coat.

The quietness of his stealth,
He stole from the falling of leaves
And the gentle breeze blowing.

Leopard snatched the smoothness of ice
And the curve of a rainbow
For his pounce.

The swiftness of his speed
Was taken from the golden eagle
Of the mountains.

At night
The blackness was stolen
And positioned in his marble eyes.

Leopard had completed his work.

Jessica Milne (10)
Sherston CE Primary School

FIRE ACROSTIC

F   ire is a volcano exploding.
I   cy water is its weakness.
R   aging fires burn down houses.
E   very fire has its flame.

Tommy Bourne (10)
Sherston CE Primary School

RHINO BEGAN

For his horns

He stole the probe of the curlew's bill
He stole the hardness of the rock
He stole the smoothness of the snake's slither

For his skin
He took the coat of an old rubber boot
He took the colour from an old man's hair
He took the strength from the gorilla's chest

For his ears
He snatched a deep cave-like tunnel
He snatched the darkness of the black hole
He snatched the coldness of the north pole

For the hump on his back
He seized the curve of the rising sun
He seized the hardness of a lump of metal
He seized the shape of crumbs dumped in a pile

For his size
He snatched the largeness of a boulder
He snatched the strength of an ox
He snatched the weight of a whale

And Rhino was made.

Adam Fitzpatrick (11)
Sherston CE Primary School

ELEPHANT BEGAN

For his ears, like flapping fans
Protecting him from the strong heat of the sun
He took two stingrays from the colossal ocean.
He took Africa's fine shape.
He took the moon and split her in half.

For his skin, like granny's wrinkles,
He took the texture of a man's leather jacket.
He took the movement of a cute baby crying.

For his immense feet, he slipped two pairs
Of enormous bootlegs on.
He took the great size of Mount Everest.
He took the weight of a blue whale, fresh from the sea.

For his trunk, like a common garden hose,
He took the length of a drainpipe.
He took the shape of a clarinet.
He took the greyness of tarmac on the road.

For his tusks, like two elegant trumpets,
He took the shape of a Maasai Kudu horn.
He took colour from white morning clouds.
He took the sleek curve of a vishing boat,
And elephant was made.

Molly Walsh (11)
Sherston CE Primary School

ELEPHANT BEGAN

To make an elephant
She took the bulk of a hill
And for her head she took a large stone
And her body was made.

For her ears
She took the shape of lettuce leaves
She took the motion of fans moving
To cool her body down.

For her tusks
She took a bent copper pipe with a shaped end
She took the whiteness of a lily flower
For the colour of her tusks.

For her trunk
She took a long dirty hosepipe
To spray over her body

For her eyes
She took two black marbles
From children in the playground.

For her feet
She took four tree trunks with the noise
Of people hammering the ground
And elephant was made.

Josie Snow (11)
Sherston CE Primary School

ELEPHANT BEGAN

To make an elephant
She took the bulk of a hill
And for her head she took a large stone.

For her ears
She took the shape of lettuce leaves,
She took the cooling of the motion of a fan.

For her tusks
She took a bent copper pipe with a sharp end
She took the whiteness of a lily flower
For the colour.

For her trunk
She snatched a long dirty hosepipe
To spray on her lovely wrinkly body.

For her eyes
She took two black marbles
From children in the playground.

For her feet
She took four vast tree trunks
With a noise of people
Hammering the ground.

And an elephant was made.

Gemma Musto (10)
Sherston CE Primary School

FIRE

Looking for disaster,
Aiming for disaster,
Cold red eyes searching
Searching for us.
For our deaths.
It has no cares,
No care for murder,
No cares for those in danger.
Blazing light, burning forests
Sparking and fizzing,
Whizzing, crackling,
Roaring, flaring
Coming to burn.
Burning houses each day
Destroying forests.
Fire is angry.

Emma Taylor (10)
Sherston CE Primary School

FIRE

Fire can be happy
Fire can be sad
When the fire meets the oil
Nobody is glad.
Fire is a dagger
That can kill you in a shot,
Fire is a sparkler burning to your hand
Never stopping, never stand,
Burning woods, burning land.

Chloe Poole (9)
Sherston CE Primary School

FIRE

Fire is completely opposite to icy
Fire is really spicy
Fire is never thirsty
Fire is bloodthirsty
Fire is a cobra coiling
Fire is hot and boiling
Fire is a rack churning
Fire is a house burning
Fire is a guillotine
Fire is a death scene
Fire will never make you cool
Fire is a blood pool
Fire is the worst death
Fire with its flamey breath
Fire is the Devil in Hell
Fire with its murderous smell
Fire is a burning flood
Fire sets off death and blood
All the animals died and bled
Don't set a fire or you'll feel quite . . . dead

Harry Pettit (10)
Sherston CE Primary School

FIRE

Fire is a burning tyre,
Fire is a burning pyre,
Fire is the biggest liar,
And I am the big admirer.
Flame is the fame of fire,
Flame is the fame of the car tyre,
Because I'm the fire.

Ben Dickenson (9)
Sherston CE Primary School

FIRE!

Fire,
Cackles and bangs as it heats up your home.
Fire,
Sizzles and then the big *bang*
As it sets off a firework.
Fire,
Snaps and then the yum!
As it heats some marshmallows.
But fire,
Burns and then the screams
As it destroys a home.
Fire,
Bubbles and gloops,
As it flows out of a volcano.
Fire is
Boiling and scalding as it completely ends a forest,
Fire is
Good and bad.

George Donaldson (10)
Sherston CE Primary School

FIRE

Fire can kill the death of people.
Fire can kill the death of animals.
Fire is your very worst nightmare.
Don't get caught by a flame of fire.
Fire burns, fire crackles
And sparks come flying out.

Don't get caught by fire.

Daniel Parkes (9)
Sherston CE Primary School

ANTELOPE BEGAN

Antelope began.
For her deftness she took
The elegance of a swan,
She took the agile movements of a flowing river.

For her sleek appearance she took
The beautiful body of a bird of prey
And the speed of a missile.

For her innocent exterior she took
The sweet smile of a child
And the colour of clear golden honey.
She took two black pendants for her huge eyes.

Last of all
The wind lent some of his freedom
And she could almost fly.

Antelope was made.

Stevie Shephard (10)
Sherston CE Primary School

FLAMES

F   lames crackle, burn, rage like the roasting sun,
L   et alone the glistening smoke like a hot cross bun,
A   massive volcano spurting out fierce red-hot lava,
M   urderous darting candles, shrinking as it burns,
E   ager, scolding, angry fire, blistering, blazing, crackling,
S   moke whirling, choking anyone who runs.

Oliver Clifton (9)
Sherston CE Primary School

ELEPHANT BEGAN

For her trunk,
She took the flexible fat hose
From a fireman.

For her ears,
She took humungous lettuce leaves
And the fanning fans to cool herself.

For her skin and colour,
She took the roughness of the ground
And the bumpy tarmac
She also took the greyness
Of a storm cloud.

For her feet and legs,
She took vast tree trunks
From the forest.

For her body,
She took a bulky side of a hill
And a sizeable bowl of gloop.

For her tusk,
She took the new moon's slender curve,
Plus a hard slice of metal.

For her movement,
She took the slow and droopy motion of a tree
Breathing in the wind.

For her voice,
She took the sound of a trumpet
Blowing in a band.

And Elephant was made!

Ellissa Sneddon-Jenkins (10)
Sherston CE Primary School

THE ORANG-UTAN BEGAN

The orang-utan began
He took his ginger hair from
The colour of an orange,

He took the giraffe's neck for
Its length of its arms and legs,

He took his motion from the
Monkey's swinging,

He took his strength from a
Weightlifter,

He took his glum face from a
Warthog's face.

He took his voice from
George of the jungle,

He took his eyes from
The blackness of night
And for his shape he
Took the letter O,

He took his grip from
A biker's gloves
And his squeeze
From a sumo wrestler,

He took the smell of rotten eggs
For the smell of his armpits,

And Orang-utan was created!

Brett Moss (10)
Sherston CE Primary School

FIRE POEMS

Fire is burning death,
It takes away your every breath,
It is a red-hot glowing blaze,
It makes you want to stare and gaze,
Water is its only fear,
It wipes it away in one big tear,
Fire is like a fiercesome beast,
The parents and children are its feast,
Fire is your very doom,
It takes you away to your grey old tomb,
Fire is an evil threat,
You and I it wants to get,
The houses and trees it will burn,
Good nor happy it will turn.

Amie Stephenson (10)
Sherston CE Primary School

FIRE

Fire is a boiling volcano just about to blow,
It is the devil's breath killing you slow,
Fire is the blazing sun shining bright,
It will hypnotise your mind, you stare in fright,
Fire is the dreadful hope in your head,
It will frighten you, it might make you dead,
Fire is the steaming heat of a demon's snarl,
It just burns your skin,
With a horrible grin.

Ross Mynes (10)
Sherston CE Primary School

FIRE POEM

Hear the evil in the air
Smell the smoke from everywhere.
See the anger in its eye
Watch it burn, watch it fry.
I dare not go too near
Because my life will be full of fear.
In the darkness it does creep
Never stops, never sleeps.
Eats on coal and eats on wood
See that horrid red-hot hood.
Burns and burns for evermore
Like a battle, like a war!
See a fire in the sky
That big ball, it never dies!

Alastair Todd (10)
Sherston CE Primary School

FEROCIOUS FIRE

Fire is a killer
Fire is a thriller
Burning, scorching
Blistering, torching
Fire is a killer.

Fire blazes
Fire comes in different sizes
Fierce, mean
Violent, keen
Fire is a killer.

Jonty Welch (9)
Sherston CE Primary School

FOG IN THE COUNTRYSIDE

Silently the fog slithers through hedges
Damp and misty
It floats over the fields and down the lanes
Houses disappear
As the blind fog swirls around them
Nothing can stop it
Hanging on every tree
Its wet dew clings to the air
Slowly it travels through the valleys
Like a mysterious, ghostly figure
Drifting through the air
Thick and wet
It slithers towards you
Silky and smooth
There is no hiding from it
It creeps through cracks
And seeps through holes in the walls
It covers the countryside in a thick mist
That only itself can clear.

Lydia McGivern (9)
The Heywood Preparatory School

MARE SERENATIS - SEA OF SERENITY

The large, exotic, colourful flowers,
Of Mare Serenatis.
The sea, like a sheet of diamonds,
With everything reflecting itself on it.
Like a portrait of the most beautiful landscape.
The swan gracefully floats across the water;
The swan dives down to kiss herself,
The picture is broken.

Charlotte Davies (11)
The Heywood Preparatory School

MORNING FOG

I wake up in the morning
To see the swirling, sweeping fog
I watch it lurk around the ground
And see cars mysteriously vanish
As the hunting fog swallows all it passes
I see a smudged, smothered glow in the distance
A ray of sunlight fighting back at the fog
The fog retreats, whirling and weaving
In and out of leaves and twigs
Slowly it turns in all directions
Wrapping around houses like a damp, grey blanket
It curves and curls, hunting all it sees
Swiftly, silently, it floats down the valley
To haunt another unsuspecting town.

Sacha Beeley (9)
The Heywood Preparatory School

NIGHT

The night is full of creeping people
And the eerie sounds from ghosts.
Shadows are like cloaks of darkness,
Long tree branches reaching to get you.
The night sky is a room of blackness,
The bats fluttering like birds of prey.
Stars are tiny gleaming lights.
The moonlight leaving a gleaming path,
For the highwayman to come.

Abigail Jackson-Wilding (9)
The Heywood Preparatory School

FOG IN THE COUNTRYSIDE

The cold, damp fog
Crosses the fields
Nothing is visible
The fields are gone
The buildings too
Everywhere you go
There is blanket of fog
It slides through barns
Sounds are muffled
By this great, grey cloud
It's lurking
Around the corner
Ready to blind
The fog is seeking me
Looking for me
Noiselessly it slithers
Down the lane
Covering everywhere
Blotting out.

David Doel (9)
The Heywood Preparatory School

OCEANUS PROCELLARUM

The stormy shadowy sea and sky
Eternal storm that'll never die
The raging sea laps the shore
The misty air swirls around
Like a whirlwind on the sea
The lightning flash
The thunder crash.

Matthew Hayes (10)
The Heywood Preparatory School

SEA FOG

Sea fog is like a ghost
That's searching for a victim
It slides across the sea
And blankets the boats
In a white cloak
Rubbing it out
Like it isn't there
It leaves the boat
And keeps on searching
For another victim
It goes into the harbour
Waiting to pounce.

William Sexton (9)
The Heywood Preparatory School

NIGHT

Frost forming like white crystals
Bubbling streams flowing
Through the moonlit forest
Stars like glittering
Stones in a ring
Willow branches dipping
Into the moonlit water
The moon shining bright
Through the frosty air
As cold as ice
But nothing disturbs the silence
Nothing disturbs the peace.

Joanne Cutler (10)
The Heywood Preparatory School

NIGHT

Deep in the forest
Dark at night
Trees sway from side to side
In the whistling wind
Their ruffled branches reaching out

The moon is a silver disc
Floating in the silent sky
Crunching leaves beneath my feet
The eyes of deer watching me

I heard a sharp sound
I stopped and stared in shock
The night was like a black sheet
Hovering above the world.

Lucinda Owen (10)
The Heywood Preparatory School

FOG

Fog moves
Floating through the air
Curving round each
And every corner
Wrapping around trees
Hanging from roofs
Slipping off doors
Blurring windows
Erasing drivers' views
Then the fog clears
As the sun burns through.

Zoe Boor (9)
The Heywood Preparatory School

THE SEA

I must go down to the sea again
To see the rushing tide come in
To hear the sounds that fill the sky
Like the cries of the seagulls

I must go down to the sea again
To smell the smells of the sea
Like the fish and the seaweed
That live in the deep blue sea

I must go down to the sea again
To climb the rough ragged rocks
To see the towering cliffs come caving in
And watch the ships come in the docks

I must go down to the sea again
To taste the big blue salty sea
Where the dangerous sharks
Come rushing in.

Sebastian Bacco (9)
Wanborough Primary School

SPELLS

Eye of dog,
Wing of bat,
Leg of frog,
Tail of cat.

Beard of goat,
Scale of fish,
Owl's coat,
Served on a dish.

Rebecca Clegg (9)
Wanborough Primary School

THE BEECH TREE

In winter the tree is sleeping
Like a prickly hedgehog hibernating.

In spring the tree awakes
And grows little green heads
On little brown twigs.

In summer the tree looks
Green and happy with its
Arms stretching to the sun.

In autumn the trees are
Sad that summer has gone away
Leaves fall like great big tears.

Isabel Salva (8)
Wanborough Primary School

MI GRANDDAUGHTER

Mi granddaughter funny,
Mi granddaughter wise.
But nobody like it when,
Mi granddaughter cries.

Mi granddaughter clever like de person who know it all,
Mi granddaughter bright like sun up in de sky.
Mi granddaughter smile like de smile on de moon,
When mi granddaughter sleep she snore but nobody know why.

Charlotte Robson (9)
Wanborough Primary School

SCHOOL DAYS

Monday is boring, it is back to school today
I can't wait until 3 then I will shout hip-hooray

Tuesday is great, we usually go for a walk
When we get back we give the older children a talk

Wednesday is better, we have lots of fun
We are on the Internet finding information

Thursday is swimming at Dorcan pool
I don't like it, the water's too cool.

Friday is the best day of the week for me
The weekend is coming, I'll have fun with my family.

Emily Smith (8)
Wanborough Primary School

WHY?

Why do I have to go to bed so early?
Why can't I have my hair long and curly?

Why do my brothers get to go round someone's house?
While I'm left to play with my little toy mouse?

Why won't my mum and dad let me have a dog?
When it could bring us to safety when we're lost in the fog!

And why is it now do you suppose,
That Dad won't tell me if he knows?

Laura Mills (8)
Wanborough Primary School

THE SEA

I must go down to the sea again,
Watching the tide come in,
Hearing the waves as they bump on the rocks,
Making a splash and a din.

I must go down to the sea again,
Building a castle with sand,
Hearing lifeguards shouting out loud,
Sitting in their towers on the land.

I must go down to the sea again,
Watching the fishing boats going by,
I love the clear water glistening:
It fills my heart with joy.

Chelsea Clegg (9)
Wanborough Primary School

MY MESSY BEDROOM

Open the door if you can
Behind it, there could be a lorry or van.
The bed I sleep in is never made,
On the floor lies a bucket and spade.
As well as bits of games including the tokens,
The chair leg is broken.
The telly is on, the music too,
Last week's lolly has turned to goo.
There is this terrible smell
Dirty underwear lies where it fell.

Ross Casey (9)
Wanborough Primary School

WHALES

Whales are the most wondrous things
They have flippers a lot like wings
Whales are the most wondrous creatures
For they have their very own water features.

Whales dip and whales dive
Yet I don't think any whales are called Clive
A whale is mightly fat not thin
And while I mention it he has no chin.

A whale swims as fast as can be
Through the great waters
Of the big wide sea.

Rachel Watts (8)
Wanborough Primary School

ONE COLD WINDY NIGHT

One cold windy night
The sound of the heating gave me a fright

One cold windy night
A golden fox had a fight

One cold windy night
I hugged my duvet really tight

One cold windy night
The breeze howled in the moonlight.

Faye Moffat (8)
Wanborough Primary School

SKATEBOARDING

W e love skateboarding
I n the skate park
C ome play with me
K eep boarding it's so cool
E xtra time to do cool tricks
D iving off the ramp with care

S kating is so fun
K eeping on the board without falling off
A t the parks learning new tricks
T he boards have got a good picture
E xtra cool wicked tricks to try out
B oarding up the wicked ramps
O ne minute left, better get going
A t 50 seconds hurry up
R amps now don't seem scary
D iving off the ramp in the air
I n the park showing off
N early finished but not to worry
G ot to go but I will be back tomorrow.

Daryll Chambers (8)
Wanborough Primary School

SPRING

S is for the sun dazzling
P is for people packing picnics
R is for rabbits hopping
I is for insects annoying everybody
N is for the nights drawing out
G is for gamboling goats

So now it's spring shout, hip hip hooray!

Jessica Heffer (9)
Wanborough Primary School

A WEEK IN OUR HOUSE

On Monday
I didn't want to go to school
My mum thinks I don't mind
I got up as . . . reluctantly as a fish leaving water.

On Tuesday
I realised I was going to piano lessons
I thought of the boring pieces I had to play
I dreaded it like . . . a cat hates water.

On Wednesday
I remembered no clubs today
I'll go to my granny's tonight
I got up as cheerfully as . . . a sunflower.

On Thursday
I think *it's only one day to the weekend*
I feel really thankful about it
I'm as energetic as . . . an athlete.

On Friday
I can't wait for PE
I hope we'll play a game of dodgeball
I'm as excited as . . . a boy at a new school.

On Saturday
I want to go down early and play on my Xbox
My favourite game is Robot Wars
I hate waiting . . . it is like waiting for a late bus.

On Sunday
I think *tomorrow it's school again*
I regret it
I'm as worried as . . . a dying man.

Duncan Hallis (8)
Winterbourne Earls School

THE MAGIC BOX
(Based on 'Magic Box' by Kit Wright)

I will place in my box . . .
An everlasting sun gleaming through the rain and clouds
A silver pallet reflecting from the golden sun
And a bronze compass with three wishes
Installed at the back.

I will insert into my box . . .
A gold medalion as light as a feather
Fifty million diamonds made out of ice
And an ice palace made out of love.

I will drop into my box . . .
The sun of the heavens
A sparkling frog from Mars
And the stars from a night so clear.

I will store in my box . . .
A sapphire dog from deep in the Earth's growth
A fireball made out of ice
And an ice cube made out of fire.

My box is constructed
Out of frog skin, wood
And the hinges are fashioned
Out of crystal made by the finest.

I shall fly to glory in a giant harrier plane
And land on a deserted island
Where no one has ever been before
It's the colour of a field full of flowers.

Tim Biles (10)
Winterbourne Earls School

MY MAGIC, MAGIC BOX
(Based on 'Magic Box' by Kit Wright)

I will place it in my box . . .
A silky silver feather that sinks in sand
The splash of a green dolphin
A gold enchanted elephant tusk.

I will hide in my box . . .
An eye from a peacock's feather
The secrets of a thousand people
And the music of ancient lands.

I will keep in my box . . .
The first blown birthday candles
The first cry and laugh of a baby
A best friend's hair.

I will put in my box . . .
A piece of fluff from a cloud
Drifting dreamboat in the bloodwaters of nightmares
A person from the year 3000.

My box is fashioned out of
A purple sun and a ginger moon
And seas and rivers on the lid and webs of secrets
It comes with hinges of a blue fire.

I shall dive to the bottom of the sea in my box
I will stare and glare in the sea
And wash up on a tropical island
With the dodo and dinosaur.

Katy Rae (9)
Winterbourne Earls School

A Week At Our House

On Monday
My mate came to my house
My house came closer and closer
It was as unnerving as . . . fighting a dragon.

On Tuesday
I had to go to school
I fell down the stairs
It was as painful as . . . falling into a volcano.

On Wednesday
I had to go swimming
I did front crawl
It was as fun as . . . playing football.

On Thursday
I played on my PlayStation 2
A Lord of the Rings game
It was as cool as . . . being a punk

On Friday
I went to my bedroom
I read a book
It was as boring as . . . standing still for one hour.

On Saturday
I had to move house
I broke a clay pigeon
It was as sad as . . . my mum dying.

On Sunday
I had to have tea
I had chicken and cabbage
It was as delicious as . . . munching a sweet.

Craig Anderson (9)
Winterbourne Earls School

A WEEK AT OUR HOUSE

On Monday
My teacher's voice echoed in my head
As I woke up
It was as scary as . . . an all night nightmare.

On Tuesday
I dread the end of the day
I dread going swimming
I fall under water like a dead fly being dropped.

On Wednesday
I *hate* coming to school
We have to do a timeline topic
It's as painful as . . . a trap.

On Thursday
I wake up in a brilliant mood
Knowing the day is going to be fab
It's as exciting as . . . buying new clothes.

On Friday
I can't wait until the morning comes
I love coming for FFK
It's as tiring as . . . running a marathon.

On Saturday
Finally I get a break
I go and rest
It's as brilliant as . . . half-term.

On Sunday
I have to go out
I have to wear my best suit
It's as boring as . . . going to school.

Rebecca Goddard (8)
Winterbourne Earls School

A WEEK IN OUR HOUSE

On Monday
I had to do my homework quickly,
I felt so tired, I felt like I was going to faint,
It was as horrid as . . . boys.

On Tuesday
It was the worst day ever, my rabbit died.
And the cereal was out of date,
It was as annoying as . . . having a broken arm.

On Wednesday
When I got out of bed my legs were aching
I really didn't want to go to school,
It was as cruel as . . . my brother.

On Thursday
I had a blocked nose all day
But when I came home we rented a video,
I was as lucky as . . . a four-leafed clover.

On Friday
I couldn't wait to get home, I was going to gymnastics
The kids and me were making up a dance,
We were as good as . . . a professional.

On Saturday
I went to West Quay to go shopping with my mum,
I bought lots of clothes.
After that we went to ASK,
It was as fun as . . . a roller coaster

On Sunday
I went to my grandma's,
I played with her cat, I had something to eat
It was as lovely as . . . a flower.

Sophie Mrozinski (8)
Winterbourne Earls School

A Week at Our House

On Monday
My mum would wake me up really early
I would have to eat my breakfast very quickly
It was as difficult as . . . staying awake all night.

On Tuesday
In the evening I go to Cubs, my Dad would bring me home
As soon as I get home I go to bed
It was as relaxing as . . . being in a hot tub.

On Wednesday
It is a plain old day
I would be forced to get out of bed early
It was as hard as . . . getting ready in a certain time.

On Thursday
I'd take my neighbour to school
I'd get to school a bit later
It was as frustrating as . . . getting all my maths wrong.

On Friday
I can't wait until football
I'd put a vest underneath my shirt
It was as quickly done as . . . a bee pollinating a flower.

On Saturday
I'd get up really late
My mum wouldn't wake me up
It was as nice as . . . being in Spain for two weeks.

On Sunday
I'd relax all day
I almost wouldn't move
It was like . . . floating on warm water.

Sam Lister (8)
Winterbourne Earls School

A WEEK IN OUR HOUSE

On Monday
I had to go to school
I had to do my homework
I had to swim a mile at swimming lessons
It was as difficult as playing on my computer games.

On Tuesday
I had to go to school
I had to get my breakfast
It was as difficult as getting out of bed.

On Wednesday
I got up to help mum with the housework
I had to hoover the carpet
It was as difficult as jumping off a plane.

On Thursday
I had to go jazz-dance
We learnt a new dance
It was as fun as jumping on a bouncy castle

On Friday
I went to school
At the end of the day I got homework
It was as difficult as pulling out a wobbly tooth.

On Saturday
I went into town
I went shopping
I bought lots of toys
It was as fun as eating a cake.

On Sunday
I went over to my friend's house
We played with her dolls
It was as fun as going swimming.

Kate Stokes (9)
Winterbourne Earls School

I WILL PLACE IN MY BOX
(Based on 'Magic Box' by Kit Wright)

I will place in my box . . .
The first day of summer
The secret of my mum's crystals
But best of all the health of my family.

I will lock in my box . . .
A season of the year
The last ever snowflake that floats into the box
But best of all my life.

I will store in my box . . .
The tusk of a newborn elephant
The tail of the tiger
But best of all the dreams of the black moon.

My box is made of bronze for the hinges
In my box I'd do my art and my crafts.

Ryan Smith (9)
Winterbourne Earls School

A WEEK AT OUR HOUSE

On Monday
It's the worst day of the week
I have to listen to my teacher, groan, groan and groan
Her voice just sticks in my head
It's as nasty as . . . my brother.

On Tuesday
I love coming to school
We do PE on Tuesday, but when I got home my dog had died
I started to cry
It was as painful as . . . a splinter.

On Wednesday
I dread the end of the day
I have to go to Judo. I really do not like it
It's as boring as . . . sitting still.

On Thursday
I get up early, I can't wait to get to school.
At the end I go to jazz dance, then I go swimming with Katherine
It's as fun as . . . a roller coaster.

On Friday
It's really exciting
Because my teacher does pupil of the week
It gives me a great day
It's as cool as . . . snowboarding.

On Saturday
I can stay in bed for longer
I love Saturday. It's the best day of the week
It's as wicked as . . . Heaven

On Sunday
It's very boring
Nothing to do. But at least I get a lie-in
It's as uncool . . . as a geek.

Jessica Clive (9)
Winterbourne Earls School

THE MAGIC BOX
(Based on 'Magic Box' by Kit Wright)

I will place in my box
A cup that doesn't hold water
A locket that is not a secret
A block of gold that is silver

I will put in my box
A cloud that does not float
A magic dog that is not magic.

I will keep in my box
An ancient card that is not ancient
A monster that is not scary
A red cat that is not red.

I will hide in my box
A feather that does not float
A boxer who does not box.

Bertie Pryer (9)
Winterbourne Earls School

A WEEK IN OUR HOUSE

On Monday
I got up late, got out of bed
My legs ached as I walked down the stairs
It was as painful as . . . falling out of a tree.

On Tuesday
I had homework to do
I tried and tried but it was too hard
It was as frustrating as . . . catching a fly.

On Wednesday
I had to go to school
I was walking down my street and almost fell asleep.
It was as tiring as . . . watching Ganddad snore.

On Thursday
I watched a movie in my bed
I really needed a drink
It was dark in the hall
It was as scary as . . . fighting a dragon.

On Friday
I was doing the cooking
It was horrible
It was as greasy as . . . swimming in a bowl of oil

On Saturday
It's finally the weekend
I can watch TV all day
It is as fun as . . . going on a go-kart ride.

On Sunday
Our family went out for dinner
I was waiting for my food
It was as boring as . . . watching EastEnders.

Kristie Johnson (9)
Winterbourne Earls School

A WEEK AT OUR HOUSE

On Monday
It's back to school
Time to get learning
It is as boring as . . . shopping.

On Tuesday
Cub time arrives
I get in the car
It is as fun as . . . a brand new bike.

On Wednesday
We go cooking mad
It's all scones and fairy cakes
It is as hot as . . .the sun.

On Thursday
It's the worst day of the week
Boring RE
It is as boring as . . . bird watching.

On Friday
It's fun FFK
And cool football
It is as cool as . . . a cucumber

On Saturday
Off I go
It's in to town
It is as fun as . . . cycling.

On Sunday
It's all relaxed
C'mon over here
It is as cosy as . . . a campfire.

Martin Brown (8)
Winterbourne Earls School

MY MAGIC BOX
(Based on 'Magic Box' by Kit Wright)

I will place in my chest . . .
The Kenyan sun, the golden moon
From an underwater world
A unicorn's horn from a faraway land.

I will lock in my chest . . .
A scale of a mermaid
A drop of blood from a golden fish
The first jewel of a spider's web.

I savour in my chest . . .
The first ever book
The golden drop of blood from a moon deer
A diamond from a pirate ship.

I will keep in my chest . . .
The feather of an angel
The purple sun from the deepest volcano
A snatch of the salty sea air.

My chest inside has the silkiest silk sewn in
My chest is carved from the smoothest willow
Its hinges are made from elephants' tusks
It's studded with jewels from faraway lands.

Then when I die
It will float up to Heaven
On a cloud's silver lining up through the stars
Up in Heaven it will rest
And will be locked forever.

Henrietta Donnelly (9)
Winterbourne Earls School

MY MAGIC BOX
(Based on 'Magic Box' by Kit Wright)

I will place in my box
The last gust of wind
The medal of an athlete
My first tooth.

I will treasure in my box
The skeleton of God
My best friend ever and the day we met
My first day at school.

I will lock in my box
A photograph of the world
My first word and step I ever made
The first blue sun and first yellow sky.

I will keep in my box
A red tree and a green hand
The time I tied my shoelace
The time I reached the age of 5.

My box is fashioned from glass
With gold stars and ruby hearts on each side
The lid is decorated with a sapphire stone
And four tiny diamonds.

I shall dance in my box
Dance on the polished wooden floor
Or I'll visit the moon
And capture a silver star of luck.

Samantha Baker (10)
Winterbourne Earls School

THE SEA

Slowly the sun is rising
The sea is nice and calm
The wind starts to blow.

The sea gets angry and
Starts to make waves
The sea is angry, it floods a nearby city
The giant waves stop.

The wind stops
The sun rises again
Everything is calm.

Another day
The sea will come
And flood your home again!

Dominique Grapin (10)
Winterbourne Earls School

THE OCEAN

The calm ocean
Is going to sleep
As the sun glitters on its body.

It shines and gleams
As the cloudless sky
Is bright and warm.

The stillness cannot be heard
Its smooth surface is not disturbed
It's like a quiet, quiet statue.

Ella Hyland (10)
Winterbourne Earls School

TURTLE

Across the ocean
Bathing on gold sand
The turtle rests
On Pacific island lands.

He lies there sleeping
Like he's dead
He seems so comfy
Without a bed.

He had a rough journey
Through giant ocean waves
Searching for food
And now sleeps on sandy bays.

Toby Shelton-Smith (10)
Winterbourne Earls School

SEA STORM

Sea scaring
Waves waving
Night nerving
Bubbles blowing
Swirling swish
Fragrance failer
Clever curving
Diving death
Easy effort
Laying late
Waiting in wait
The sea, the sea.

Rachel Miller (10)
Winterbourne Earls School

THE SEA IS ALIVE

Dolphins dodging through the waves,
Salty star swimming.
Massive blue whales in a pool,
Great white sharks hunting,
Fishes swimming round and round,
Now an eight-legged octopus.

On the top of this parade,
Ships, ships and more ships,
Red, green and blue
The sunshine burning down, sweltering hot,
Feel the water warm.
Who could imagine one big thing
Carries so much inspiration,
The sea, it's alive, the sea, it's alive!

Alexandra Rose Williams (10)
Winterbourne Earls School

PANDA

Bold, bashing black is my colour
White, well and white are my patches
Bulging bamboo sticks is what I eat
With watery, warty bugs as well
Vegetarian is what I am
China is where I live
By the water I do hide
In the ranging rocks, from the sky
I want to live peacefully in my home
Please help me or I will be extinct.
Forever!

Lily-Mae Richardson (9)
Winterbourne Earls School

GERMAN SHEPHERD

My tail is super scruffy
My patches permanently brown and black
I like . . .
Super squashy sticks
Digging deep dens
Catching crafty cunning cats
But my most favourite things to do are
Surfing seas as long as light
Catch the flying filthy fishes
And then I like to go home
Have my comfortable warm soft belly rub
Have a quick dry
All before I settle down
For bed!

Emily Vaughan (10)
Winterbourne Earls School

ME!

I'm an under, over, mixed up clout,
A little girl that screams and shouts.
If there's a spot of trouble I'm in
I really make an awful din.
I'm an inside, outside little girl,
And when I'm angry I unfurl.
My favourite thing is reading in bed
And lying down, resting my head.
I really can't take second best,
I have to be on top of all the rest.
But I'm an under, over, mixed up clout,
A little girl that screams and shouts.

Bethany Miller (10)
Winterbourne Earls School

A WEEK IN OUR HOUSE

On Monday
I woke up early
My mum was having a shower
She was as wet as . . . a wet dog.

On Tuesday
I played on the PlayStation
The game I played was hard
It was like . . . running a marathon.

On Wednesday
I went to a friend's house
We played hide-and-seek
It was like . . . being Robin Hood.

On Thursday
I played on my castle
It was great fun.
It was like . . . an exciting game on my PlayStation.

On Friday
I played with my friends
The swimming pool we played in
Was as deep as . . . a river.

On Saturday
I trained by climbing trees
It was difficult
It was like . . . climbing an extremely long rope.

On Sunday
I rested all day
I felt very comfortable
It was like . . . being lowered onto an enormous cushion.

Oliver Blakeman (9)
Winterbourne Earls School